TIRED OF TRYING TO MEASURE UP

TIRED OF TRYING TO MEASURE UP

Jeff VanVonderen

BETHANY HOUSE PUBLISHERS
MINNEAPOLIS, MINNESOTA 55438

The Bible text in this publication is from the Revised Standard Version of the Bible, copyrighted 1946, 1952, © 1971, 1973 by the Division of Christian Education of the National Council of the Churches of Christ in the USA, and used by permission.

Scripture quotations marked NASB are from the New American Standard Bible, © The Lockman Foundation 1960, 1962, 1963, 1968, 1971, 1972, 1973, 1975, 1977.

Copyright © 1989
Jeff VanVonderen
All Rights Reserved

Published by Bethany House Publishers
A Ministry of Bethany Fellowship, Inc.
6820 Auto Club Road, Minneapolis, Minnesota 55438

Printed in the United States of America

Library of Congress Cataloging-in-Publication Data

VanVonderen, Jeffrey.
    Tired of trying to measure up / Jeff VanVonderen.
        p. cm.

    1. Grace (Theology) 2. Freedom (Theology) 3. Shame.
4. Christian life—1952–   I. Title.
BT761.2.V36   1989
234—dc20   89–38883
ISBN 1–55661–030–0   CIP

Dedicated to the folks at The Christian and Missionary Alliance Church of the Open Door in Minneapolis, Minnesota. They are willing to risk admitting that they are tired. They share their wounds aloud with God and with one another, and are no longer willing to settle for anything or anyone but Jesus.

Special thanks to my wife Holly and my four daughters Callie, Jesi, Erin, and Kara. In the most important ways my projects are really family projects. I couldn't do them without my family's love and understanding.

Books by Jeff VanVonderen

Families Where Grace Is in Place
Good News for the Chemically Dependent
The Subtle Power of Spiritual Abuse (with David Johnson)
Tired of Trying to Measure Up
When God's People Let You Down

Table of Contents

Part I

——

Wounded by Shame

Introduction

Why Can't I Measure Up?

If Christianity is supposed to be a life filled with joy and meaning, why do I always feel as if I'm struggling—and tired of it? Why do I feel so guilty? Why is it so hard for me to rest, even when I need to? Why can't I stop all of my religious activity, even though it long ago ceased to be a joy? Why do I find myself repeating patterns I vowed I never would?

Do you, like hundreds of people who have come to me for pastoral counseling, ever ask these questions? Do you feel like you're slogging knee-deep through mud? Like you *never* measure up?

If so, then perhaps you will find the help you need in these chapters. I'm *not* offering you "ten helpful steps" on how to get yourself, friends, or family members to behave in a "Christian" manner. If trying hard were the key to the victorious Christian life, you'd probably be in the Hall of Fame by now! You don't need to learn more ways to try hard. Personal and pastoral discoveries have convinced me that Christians need to learn how to *rest*.

Tired of Trying to Measure Up springs from personal experience and concern over a frightening phenomenon. The great majority of the people I see in counseling are struggling with being tired. Not sleepy tired. They are emotionally, psychologically drained. More than that, they are *spiritually* tired, which is the most debilitating kind of "tired." And it seems to me that most of the literature, seminars, sermons and counseling available to Christians have one thing in common: They give already-tired people something more to *do*, which is exactly what they do *not* need. "Come to me, all of you who are weary and overburdened, and I will give you rest!" (Matt. 11:28, Phillips). Jesus' response to tired people is rest.

If "rest" sounds rather foreign to you, an idea too unrealistic or too good to be true, then somewhere in your life you've probably been

11

involved in relationships that were based on "conditions." I have learned, by talking with countless folks who are weary from their inner struggles, that most often, loving acceptance was held out like a carrot on a string—the tiniest "taste" dependent on their "good enough" performance, which never quite measured up.

Perhaps you, too, can still feel the lure of those dangled, emotional "carrots." Unwritten expectations and rules gave you a sense of shame that you as a person are unacceptable. Perhaps you are still draining away your emotional and spiritual strength as you try constantly to measure up to standards that are higher than you can reach. These standards may have become so deeply ingrained that you are not even aware of them, let alone conscious of how to get free from their tyranny.

My purpose is to shine a light on the hurtful messages you once received that still play over and over like a tape recording in your soul. I want to help you recognize the source of those messages, what they *say*, and what they *mean*. I want to help you break away from unrealistic standards and leave them behind. I believe you will come to understand your life patterns—patterns you may hate but can't seem to "will" yourself out of, patterns that make you weary.

At some point in our lives, each one of us struggles with wounds from hurtful relationships. Some people have been hurt more than others. Some struggle more than others. As you read on in this book, areas of your pain will be exposed and identified. The first step to healing is finding the wounds, and sometimes *finding* them hurts. I wish this were not so.

But here's the good news—God loves you *for free*. You have nothing to purchase or prove, no one to impress. What Jesus says about you is your "bottom line." You are loved, accepted and not alone. You are considered worthwhile and capable—by the King of the Universe! What else, *who* else matters? Healthy behaviors *result* from an identity that's healthy and fully based upon God's performance on our behalf. You can learn to perform *out of* the fullness that is yours in Christ. While you're on the way to discovering that abundant life, it's okay to start asking, "Why do I do what I do?" You can also begin learning to rest because your identity—who you *are*—is settled in Christ. Your acceptance and value is settled. As a recipient of God's grace, you have the resources you need in order to change. But, equally important, because of that grace you can take the time you need to do so.

That really is Good News!

1

How It All Began

The ancient myths tell of a man who was punished by the gods. They bound him and cursed him with a burning thirst, then held up a cup of cool water before him. But no matter how he struggled, the ropes merely cut deeper into his flesh and the soothing water remained a few tantalizing inches beyond his parched lips. *Pagan*, you say? What does that have to do with us today—and especially with Christians?

In my ministry as a pastoral counselor, I meet with countless men and women, young people and old, who are weary from their own struggle against invisible bonds. They see before them the promises Jesus made to all His followers: ". . . whoever drinks of the water that I shall give him will never thirst; the water that I shall give him will become . . . a spring of water welling up to eternal life" (John 4:14). "I am come that [you] might have life, and that [you] might have it more abundantly" (John 10:10b, KJV).

"What's wrong with me?" a lot of these folks ask. "I know what the gospels say. And I've committed my life to Christ. But no matter how hard I try, I never seem to measure up."

For some, it's a matter of trying to stop sinful and damaging behaviors, only to find themselves falling again and again. Others have a sense that they have given all they can give, served all they can serve—and still something's wrong. They feel defective. Some have gone off into obvious sin, found themselves more bitter and empty than ever, and then tried to come back to their faith for one more weary "go" at it. Most have been worn down with trying so hard, while the abundant flow of living water that was promised is still tantalizing inches beyond the reach of their dry, thirsty souls.

"The worst part of it," some tell me, "is that I can't talk to my pastor or Christian friends about this emptiness. They'll give me one more 'formula' to follow, and I'm already too tired of trying."

If you are one of these folks, I want to assure you: Hope *is* within your reach! And you don't even have to embark upon a new program of spiritual push-ups and jumping-jacks.

That's not just good news—it's great news! How well I know, because I went through the same kind of struggle myself. And I discovered the problem that lies at the root of our battle—it's called *shame.*

When You Have to Measure Up

When I was a young Christian—all of seventeen—I had no way of knowing that I was about to turn away from almost everything I believed in—from all that people saw of me from the outside. At that time, in fact, I was president of my church youth group and avoided the guys who looked and acted like I would—just a few years later. But time was not the only factor: there was a deep, massive void within me. I could actually feel it sometimes, but didn't know what it was.

You see, I grew up in a small farming community in northeastern Wisconsin, where my family attended an independent, strong fundamentalist church. Like many churches or Christian groups, ours had a definite character: guys wore their hair a certain length; girls knew that hemlines and necklines didn't rise above or fall below certain limits. There were acceptable things you just did, and unacceptable things you just didn't do. Even though my folks were a little less demanding about these standards, I seemed to thrive in this environment. In fact, when it came to measuring up, I was a real trophy.

There was a nursing home near our town: I visited the people there regularly. There were Bible verses to be memorized: I could rapid-fire them aloud by the dozen. If I'd worn all my perfect attendance pins from Sunday school on the same day, I'd have touched off every metal detector within a 50-mile radius. My goal was to be the best, most positive person I could be.

There were, however, some "cracks" in my performance. Like the fact that, inside, I really wanted to stay home and watch Walt Disney on Sunday evenings instead of attending church. Or the fact that I could never wait to get out of that nursing home, with its medicinal-smelling old people. And no one else knew that I'd only run for youth group president because I thought it would attract the attention of the girls. But I thought that if I kept at it long enough, I'd acquire a taste for all these good things. Maybe the worst part was that, inwardly, no matter how much I did, I still had the sense that God was disappointed in me. I couldn't have put it into words, but it was like waiting for someone to tell me I'd fulfilled an unwritten quota and could take a breather—or like waiting for the empty spaces inside to fill in.

There was one skill I did acquire by the time I left home for college: how to please people. I learned how to "read" any group I was with and determine what the standards were that would gain my acceptance. During my four years of college and a brief stint in the army, I learned that each group—whether a family, church, or social clique—had its own standard of acceptance. So I found myself striving to earn the same sense of being "special" from any new company I was keeping. There was just one big problem: The standards had changed dramatically from what I had known.

In order to "make it" in college and with my army buddies, I had to be the worst, most negative-type person I could be. At first it was kind of bewildering to me to discover that I had so little inner strength, so little sense of individual identity— and pitifully little resistance to falling in with what everyone else was doing. After all, I *had* been a youth leader.

By the time I reached my early twenties, I had a full-blown addiction to drugs and alcohol. I was sick and tired of "doing good," so I gave up entirely. I burned out my physical body, not to mention my money, family and friends. I'd become the total opposite of everything I'd stood for—in just a few short years. I no longer even tried to understand why all the good things I'd done—all those scriptures I'd planted in my brain, and all the commitments I'd made to God—had so little power to keep me from sinking into this mess.

I decided it had to be something about me. There was some kind of defect that had been there all along and was just now coming out. If Christianity could be compared to an assembly line, then I was a reject on God's conveyor-belt. Whatever I'd done to be a good Christian, it hadn't been enough to keep me that way. I was at the lowest point of my life.

I won't go into all the external details of what brought me to a major turning point one night; those are important only to me. It's what took place on the inside that matters—the peace and completeness that began to filter in after all those years of struggle.

As Christians, you and I might be quick to say that I finally came to repentance. By that, we normally would mean that I made a 180-degree turn away from sin and bad behavior, and started behaving like a Christian again. But that's not exactly what happened.

The truth is, the prospect of once again becoming a pillar in the religious community and starting to perform in a positive way left the taste of dust in my mouth. It felt like going back to prison. Besides that, I knew it wouldn't work. I'd been good and positive in the first place, and that only wore me down; it gave me no real life inside. No, that night I saw something else.

The first thing I came face-to-face with was my deep, abiding sense of defectiveness, which now I would identify as a sense of shame.

Let me clarify something. Shame is often confused with guilt. But they're not the same. God created you and me so that when we do something wrong we experience a sense of guilt. Guilt is like a spiritual nerve-response to sin, an emotion in response to wrong behavior ("I acted in a way that was wrong, and I feel guilty"). Those uncomfortable impulses that stab our conscience are meant to turn us away from the wrong we're doing and turn us back to God. In that sense, guilt is a healthy thing. Because guilt comes as a result of something you and I do, we can do something about it—change our behavior—and the guilty feeling will go away.

Shame, on the other hand, is not just a feeling, though we often speak of it that way ("You ought to feel ashamed of yourself"). Shame is the belief or mindset that something is wrong with you. It's something you can live with and not necessarily be aware of it. It's not that you feel bad about your behavior, it's that you sense or believe you are deficient, defective or worthless as a human being.

Consequently, you develop a shame-based way of looking at yourself. You accept the view that others might slip up and make mistakes once in a while, but they're still basically worthwhile people. You, however, are like a mirror image of that: No matter how many times you get it right (whatever it is, according to the standards of your environment) you will never be acceptable. Down deep, you believe something is wrong with you.

Because you and I are not isolated persons, we can also build shame-based systems. A shame-based system can be a family, a school, a church, or Christian group in which the authority figures demand a certain level of performance, whether spoken or implied. If you don't live up to the standard of the system, messages that are either subtle or overt will tell you that you are not good enough—you simply do not measure up ("Shame on you!").

But that's not even the saddest part.

The Worst of All

Worst of all, a sense of shame can keep you at a distance from God. It keeps you from praying because, "Why would God want to hear from someone like me?" Or, if He does incline His ear (condescendingly), why would He answer? "I don't come close to living up to His standards. He doesn't really want to answer my prayers. He doesn't even want to be around me. At best, I'm just a spiritual stepchild."

After realizing the sense of shame I'd had for so long, the second thing I saw on the night my life began to change was this: All my life- -and mostly without even knowing it—I'd been trying to measure up to the standards of other people, including my own family and my Christian environment.

Even tougher, I'd been trying to live up to the standards of an utterly holy God who, I was so often reminded, could not tolerate even one whiff of sin. Hadn't He laid the sins of the whole world on His own Son on the cross, and then turned His face away? If that was true, I'd thought, then God's stomach must turn every time He even thought about me with all the secret sins and inconsistencies in my life.

Living with that continuous sense of shame, I'd entered into a process that involved three steps: trying, trying harder, and trying my hardest. Did I say three steps? Actually, there were four: I gave up— or at least I switched the standards by which I was trying to measure myself. True, the alcohol and drugs could have killed me physically, but to be honest, even though I had been a Christian, I was already nearly dead inside.

The solution to my pattern of living was not to repent—that is, it wasn't to start over and begin to live a good life. No, the solution was found in something else—something that tasted like cool clear water to my soul; and it tasted like life.

It was freedom from shame! Wouldn't you like a drink from the same well?

Take a Good Look

Have you ever felt like you were almost at the end of yourself?

You'd tried so hard to be good—to do the right thing, not the wrong thing—only to fail, for—what was it?—the ten-thousandth time? And even if you'd made yourself believe God forgave you 9,999 times, surely this was the one that tipped the scales.

Or maybe for you it's just the opposite. You've been the best Christian mom, dad, son, daughter, Sunday school teacher, youth leader, or pastor. You read your Bible, pray, tithe faithfully—but you have yet to lay your finger on the one button that's going to make God smile.

Some women strive to keep the neatest home, have the best-behaved kids and have the most neatly-pressed-and-creased husband on the block. Others try to keep themselves a step ahead of the men at the office. But there's always one more smudge, an embarrassing volley of sibling name-calling in front of guests, and always one more wrinkle. And then some man always takes the credit for your good work at the office.

Many men shadow-box their way through life: pastors fall into the "I-and-my-flock-must-become-more-'on-fire'-for-Christ" trap; businessmen become slaves to the race for a more prestigious job, a better home in a more exclusive community—with the nagging question as to why each milestone was supposed to be so important, or why it's not enough once they've reached it.

Do you feel like you want to call it quits? Maybe you've even tried giving up for a while—just long enough to give yourself a pep talk, or a brow-beating. You struggle to your feet—you can hardly believe it—one more time! After all, didn't your mom or dad tell you, "Nobody likes a quitter"? You begin to hardly recognize yourself.

In order to understand the deep effects shame has on an individual, it's necessary to go through a process—one that's similar to cutting through the layers of a flower bulb to expose the living core. We'll have to look at the answers to some questions, such as:

- To what extent has your personality been shaped by a sense of shame?
- To what degree have your views about life and other people been affected?
- How much does a sense of shame limit you—dictating what you do or don't do?
- Has shame caused you to become a victim, always at the mercy of people who are demanding, authoritative?

The first step toward a new life is to gather up all those fragments of confusing thoughts and actions and examine them in a new light. You will discover how a sense of shame took control in the first place. Only then can you see how to loosen its hold.

For now, let's begin with a deeper look inside of you.

2

What's Wrong With Me?

"God feels so far away most of the time. In fact, I feel guilty saying I'm a Christian because I'm such a bad one, really. I can't even read my Bible anymore. Every time I open it I feel so guilty I can't stand it. I used to like reading it. What's wrong with me?"

"I don't get it. I work like crazy to get my job situation turned around. And when it's finally working, I do something to ruin it. And I do this over and over again. What's wrong with me?"

"I want so badly to have a lasting relationship with a man. But whenever things start to get serious, I get petrified and find some way to run away. Am I going to be alone forever? What's wrong with me?"

Although the wounded people quoted above all *sound* different, they're really just reciting different verses of the same song: the sad song of shame. Through the years, I've noticed certain common characteristics and behavior patterns in many of the people who come for counseling. Most feel a profound sense that they are the only ones with their particular struggle.

Perhaps it's best to begin describing some of the struggles I've encountered. You may find that some or even most of the following characteristics apply to you. I'm sure the following list isn't complete. More than that, I want you to see from the outset that you're not *alone* after all.

Carefully consider each of the following traits.

Do You Feel or Think This Way?

The first group of traits concerns how you relate to yourself:

You have a "shame-based" identity. By my definition, that means you suffer from low self-esteem, or a negative self-concept. You base your assessment of yourself on the "fact" that you are a bad person,

19

defective, inadequate, unlovable, undeserving. Even if no one else criticized you, you would call yourself a bad person.

You are highly performance-conscious. A man who came to my office recently said, "Anything worth having in life is worth working for." But you can't *work* for God's acceptance! The only way to get life, value and acceptance from God is to accept it as a free gift. *He* must do the work for us to get what is worthwhile.

You don't know yourself very well. When you come from relationships that make you feel ashamed because you have *needs, feelings, opinions,* or *struggles,* you can become so out-of-touch with your own needs that you often don't even know what they are. When you do become aware of a need, you scold yourself for being selfish or undeserving.

You are frequently unaware of your own feelings. Because the expression of feelings was frowned upon, you have learned to hide or ignore yours. You've become an expert at "stuffing them"; simply because feeling *hurts* too much. However, feelings are a fact. Not *showing* them isn't the same as not *having* them. Emotions are so much a part of who you are—but being *unaware* of your feelings prevents you from making wise choices in response to them. You're controlled by feelings in a way you probably don't recognize. That is, you do everything possible to avoid stressful situations and keep peace, but you always seem to find yourself in the midst of conflict anyway.

You have a tendency to be idolatrous. Many people who have missed out on their parents' blessing (the message that is directly opposite the shaming message) look for that lost love in all the wrong places . . . in an attempt to try to meet legitimate needs in an illegitimate way.[1] This is idolatry. Idolatry means basing your sense of life, value, and acceptance on something other than God. Your view of yourself, your moods, and your sense of value depends on externals— that is, on people's opinion of you, on clothes, money, a relationship, your behaviors (religious or otherwise), your children's behaviors, and a host of other things besides God's acceptance. Idolatry *is* graven images and pagan rituals; but it is also allowing what the neighbors think to control your actions.

You have a high level of anxiety. Things change. People change. Circumstances change. Since your sense of well-being comes from things that are totally up for grabs (people's opinions, your ability to

---

[1]Gary Smalley and John Trent, *The Blessing* (Thomas Nelson, 1986), 145.

keep everyone happy, the interest rates, your job, doing enough at church), you often feel anxious. It's like building a house on sand, and as you pound the last nail a raindrop hits you on the nose. You *know* what happens to houses built on sand, so it's no wonder you're anxious!

You are wounded. You can't recover from problems you aren't "supposed" to have. You can't benefit from struggles you "shouldn't" be going through. You can't get help for problems you "can't" talk about. But concealing your wounds isn't the same as not having them. Consequently, you've been shamed out of talking about your problems; therefore, you're still being affected by them.

You are tired. In order to make it in a shame-based system, you had to acquire certain skills or become an expert at a certain role that was conducive to survival. Survival is a lot of work. Now you're stuck using skills that worked to get you through your past but don't work in present relationships. Maybe you learned to be perfect and perform at your best all the time—and now when it's time to rest you can't, even though your hyperactivity is hurting you and the ones you love. Or maybe your way of surviving was to pretend that things really didn't matter that much. Now you can't seem to get past a feeling of hopelessness or apathy that makes it hard to get motivated.

The following traits deal with how you relate to others:

You are unaware of personal "boundaries." Boundaries are those invisible barriers that tell others where they stop and where you begin. Personal boundaries notify others that you have the right to have your own opinion, feel your own feelings and protect the privacy of your own physical being. It's okay to expect others to respect your boundaries.

For instance, it's okay to not follow or even listen to the advice of another who expects you to receive it just because it's offered. It's also okay to ask for advice if you want it. It's okay for my thirteen-year-old daughter to NOT want me even NEAR the bathroom when she's in it, even though I used to change her diapers. She is establishing a personal boundary she has a right to have. She also has a right to expect me to respect it. People who have been shamed don't know they have the right to set personal boundaries. Shame-based systems (relationships that communicate condemning messages) have told them that they're selfish to have private limits. Aggressively abusive people may have crossed your boundaries without permission, thereby obliterating those restrictions. At the very least, you were not allowed to say no. It has been "okay" for people to *control* your life because they were your parents, spouse, leader, a male, or some other person that supposedly had "the right."

I've counseled women who have been victims of rape. None of them say, "I'm *important,* and I don't deserve to be treated that way." More often they say, "*I* should have known better than to have been there at that time or to have dressed that way." They have no sense of their right to boundaries. It's as if they think their location or what they wear gives someone else the right to violate their physical boundaries.

You have incredible "radar." When you grow up in a place where the main preoccupation is external behavior and how things *look,* you become an expert at noticing how things look. Most likely, you can walk into the middle of a situation and after no time at all know exactly who's in charge and what that person expects from you. Since it's been your job to keep everyone satisfied or at peace (except yourself), you've become an expert at reading people's nonverbal signals and following the unwritten dictates. You are constantly ready to adjust yourself in order to keep someone happy or to earn his approval.

You feel as if you don't belong. You can be in a room full of people and feel lonely, as if no one knows or cares that you're there. It would just be easier for you if you could leave.

You can't tell what normal is. When you live in a world of unwritten rules, the emphasis is placed on appearances and not on the underlying truth or reality of the situation. You behave as if you are normal, without having a sound basis for making that decision. You live in a world that you created all your own, a world of what life would be like *if* . . . What your home would be like *if* . . . The way your parents would relate to each other *if* . . . The things that would be possible *if* . . .[2] Since the thing that matters is how things look and not what's *real,* you've lost track of what real is. Trying to discover what is real is a messy process involving much trial and error. In many churches and families error is not permissible, and people are shamed for trying to deal with reality. Reality must be stopped. Maybe you've been surprised at times by the fact that every family in the whole world doesn't do things the way your family did. Some of those families are even *happy!*

You have a difficult time trusting people. Trust is a confidence in the fact that you're not going to be hurt by someone. But you've been

---

[2]Janet G. Woititz *Adult Children of Alcoholics*, (Health Communications, Inc., 1983), 26–27.

hurt so much; the relationships that were supposed to be the safest were the least safe. People who were supposed to be the most dependable were the least dependable. Those who were to have protected you from the perpetrators of pain *were* the perpetrators. Now, it's hard for you to trust that you *won't* be hurt. Moreover, you've grown to trust that you *will*.

You are afraid of being deserted. In many families and churches, people are not available emotionally, spiritually, or even physically. Perhaps where you grew up, people were not dependable. Closeness was nonexistent. Relationships were full of strings, and you couldn't count on anyone. Now, when someone close to you chooses to pursue his own needs or likes, you see it as his effort to leave you behind. You're secretly terrified that you'll be abandoned. Once you *have* someone, you hang on for dear life.

Do You Do This?

If you have had relationships in the past, or presently are involved in relationships that give you a sense of shame or blame, you most likely interpret life through a "shame-grid." A shame-grid causes you to receive words, external circumstances and events, and the way others treat you as an indictment—a judgment that you aren't good enough as a person. You interpret words and actions to mean more than what they really mean; in other words, you readily assume that people see you as a lesser person.

For instance, if a person states his opinion and I disagree, what that means is, "He has an opinion; I have an opinion; and the two are not the same opinion." Simple and straightforward. When my disagreement filters through his shame-grid, however, what he *hears* is this: "Jeff thinks something is wrong with *me* for having my opinion."

Let me illustrate further: "I don't agree with you" translates: "You're stupid for thinking that way."

Making a mistake translates: "I am less of a person."

Spilling your milk translates: "I'm a klutz."

Someone else having a number of positive circumstances (a promotion, a new car, finding a spouse) translates: "God must not love me as much as them."

Your children's misbehaving translates: "I'm a lousy parent."

Your inability to live up to some "Christian formula" translates: "I'm a defective Christian."

Your spouse's feeling sad translates: "I'm a poor husband/wife."

Your parents' being upset translates: "I'm a failure as their child."
The following traits make up your shame-grid:

You use a lot of negative "self-talk." Whenever your performance doesn't measure up to the standard, you speak to yourself like the prosecuting attorney in a case in which you are also the defendant! You step outside of yourself, turn around, stick your finger in your face and let the accusations fly. "What's wrong with me? How could I be so stupid?" or "How could I have thought someone as nice as that could ever like someone as worthless as me?" You tell yourself, "It doesn't matter what I feel," or "Nobody cares what happens to me," or "I'm useless." People make poor choices sometimes and can't do everything perfectly, but notice that these phrases are about you and your worth as a person, not about your behaviors.

You don't allow yourself to make mistakes (or admit them). When you've been taught that performance is the way to be valuable and acceptable, mistakes bring shame. They document imperfection. Therefore, any personal performance that doesn't measure up to "the standard of perfection"—whatever that is to you—must be denied, explained, justified, minimized, rationalized, or blamed on someone else.

You are overresponsible. If there's a problem, *you* must have caused it (even though you're not sure how). If there's a crisis, you're supposed to solve it (even though the past has taught you that you'll probably fail). It's your job to make sure everyone else is happy, that no one is disappointed, that their needs are met, and that the whole world is at peace.

You martyr your own needs. Your shame-grid tells you that needing something means you are being selfish. You interpret neediness to mean that you're not adequate for every task. "To do without" is a virtue. You can express a need only if you're *really* suffering. Otherwise, tough it out. ("You should be grateful that you didn't grow up during the depression.") This equation defines your life experience:
SHAME + LACK OF BOUNDARIES + PERFORMANCE FOCUS = MARTYR.
In other words, you feel *dead.*

You don't trust your "radar." Earlier, I described your incredible radar. Unfortunately, being shamed for noticing things has taught you not to trust your radar. In other words, you've learned to think that you are the problem for thinking there's a problem! Therefore, the information gathered by your incredible radar gets filtered by your shame-grid and comes out, "It can't really be that bad. It must be *me.* I must have a critical spirit."

Now we come to the way you relate to your own life. As a result of living behind a shame-grid, some or all of the following traits my apply:

You set up inappropriate boundaries. Coming from a shaming environment where you lacked a sense of having a right to your own boundaries, as well as lacking opportunities to practice setting up personal boundaries, has led to present problems. It has resulted in not putting up boundaries where needed and putting them up where not needed. You allow people who are close to you to continue to hurt you but protect yourself from those who are safe.

You act like a victim. People with a history of relationships that have given them a sense of shame often become victims in later-life relationships because of the deeply ingrained message that they are "defective." When they experience rape, incest, physical, emotional or spiritual abuse, neglect, job intimidation, or they are simply taken advantage of, these events shout a message through their shame-grid that gets through loud and clear: You lack a boundary that says, "I don't have to be treated this way." You don't have a *no* for an answer!

You tend to "code" when you communicate. Growing up with the potential for shame every time you open your mouth creates the need to code. You make it hard for people to confront you, because you don't say what you mean outright. Since it's not okay to have needs, or notice things, or break unwritten rules, then you have to say and do things in code. Otherwise they may respond by saying, "You're wrong to feel that way," which will "prove" to you that you *are* wrong.

For instance, perhaps you may have lived with unwritten rules like these: "It's selfish to have needs," or "If you have to ask for something it doesn't count if you get it." You listened to people speak "in code." When someone *really* wanted to get his needs met, he said, "Oh, you don't have to go through all of that trouble for *me*." This translates, "If you really want to please me, you'll do it!" Someone who doesn't think he has a right to an opinion might say, "Oh, don't you think it would look better this way?" Translated, this means, "I think it *would* look better this way." A person who says, "God helps those who help themselves" might really be saying, "I feel *selfish* if I ask for help," or "I don't *deserve* anyone's concern." Or he might be saying, "Something's wrong with me if I need help."

You suffer a lot of stress-related illness. This is just the end result of the process of trying to live a "perfect" life. Being perfect is hard work. Also, your shame-history has left you with many skills that help you *avoid* problems, but without the skills you need to *face* and *solve* problems. Since avoiding doesn't solve, you get to keep the problems—and the related stress.

You can't have guilt-free fun. In your book, fun is a waste of valuable time. You could be doing something "meaningful"—like fixing, or straightening, or putting something away. Perhaps the real reason you can't have fun is because your childhood was stolen from you. During that time of life when you were supposed to be learning about fun, anything other than seriousness and perfection brought shame. You were expected to act like an adult: It wasn't okay for you to be a kid, because kids aren't perfect; they act weird sometimes (and "what would people think?"). Now you're an uptight adult and don't know why.

During the last conversation I had with my dad before his death, I asked him if there were things in his life he wished he could do over again. He said there were three. First, he wished he would have gone to army officers' candidate school instead of staying in the infantry with his cousin. Second, he wished he wouldn't have run for the school board. (He believed that to be the cause of the ulcers which developed eventually into his fatal cancer.) And third, he said, "I wish I would have let myself enjoy your kids more—and let them be kids." This was the one that brought tears to his eyes. And to mine, as well.

It's true, some grandpas play with their grandkids, teaching them about birds or plants or airplanes, joke with them, or just enjoy watching them. My dad spent a lot of his time with my kids—fixing, correcting, or shaming them. And when they couldn't act "adult" enough he avoided them. Now that he's gone, they're left with only two positive memories of fun times with my dad.

You act in ways that seem contradictory. For a period of time you're the perfectionist, worried about what people think. Then you become a slob, and you couldn't care less. You try hard, then give up. In part this has to do with energy level. When your "self-effort fuel level" is high, you're on a try-hard trip. When your juice runs out, you have to rest. But since it's not okay to need to rest, you have to treat things as if they really don't matter. You blot them out of your thinking during that time.

The same imbalance is true in other areas of particular concern to you. You may be totally engrossed in a relationship with someone, then apathetic; you can never just relax. You diet or gorge—never just eat in a healthy, balanced way. You're either engulfed in church work, or hiding from the Sunday school superintendent—never just moving steadily within God's reasonable agenda for you. Emotionally, you're up and down—either skyrocketing, or on a downward plummet.

Sometimes both sides of the contradiction happen at the same time. This is really confusing to everyone involved—you included. Perhaps you've heard something like this from a person close to you: "Sometimes I feel as if you're beckoning me to come near with one hand and pushing me away with the other." This kind of mixed signal we might dub the "come close/stay away" gesture. You ask for intimacy and then push it away when it comes. You signal that you want help, then give a "hands-off" message. Relationships are very hard for you. They scare you. They feel like a nasty trick waiting to be played.

You can't deal with gifts very well. First, you can't *receive* gifts. If you're a shame-based person, there are two ways to shame you. One is simply to say outrightly, "You're a terrible person; why don't you dry up and blow away?" The second is to give you a gift—for free. If I give you a free gift, it attacks your shame-grid, which reminds you that you don't deserve a gift, or makes you suspect that I must really want something in return. "There must be a string attached," you say. Or, "If you knew what I'm really like, you'd never be giving me this gift." You'll have to think of a way to pay me back immediately, or the gift will drive you nuts.

Secondly, you can't *give* gifts. You have to be careful that you don't give away too much without keeping track, always making sure people notice, or pay you back. If you just give and give and give, you might run out. Maybe your Aunt Ethel gives you a wall plaque for your birthday. If you don't care for it, you may sell it at your next garage sale. Two years later, your aunt visits you and says, "Where's that plaque I gave you? I suppose you didn't really like it . . ." She says this with a sigh and a little whine in her voice. You've just discovered that it wasn't really a gift. It had a string attached, and Ethel is tugging on it hard. But whose gift was it—hers, or yours?

When you give a gift, it belongs to the person to whom you gave it. It's not yours anymore. Keeping track of a gift is a contradiction. Noticing you didn't get a gift in return is also a contradiction. Often people offer to pay for each other's lunch, *not* because they want to, but because it's easier than accepting someone's gift. Their offer isn't a genuine expression of caring; it's a way to not feel *obligated*. (Remember, if you and I ever go out to lunch, don't offer to pick up the bill unless you mean it. I've learned to accept gifts quite well!) This is a VERY serious problem when it comes to the idea of receiving the gift of unconditional love from God and others. Charles Solomon says that the impaired ability to give or receive love is the most pervasive trait present in the clients with whom he works.[3]

You sabotage your own success. At the same time that you are seeking the acceptance of others—the way someone who's dying searches for water in the desert—when you finally get it, it collides against every deeply ingrained message of shame. Feeling good feels bad.

I'm convinced there are people in therapy who *could* get well— but they don't because *well* people are expected to be responsible for their actions. Dysfunction is simply safer. Why? Because failure based on illness seems less shameful than failure without an excuse. As a kid, do you remember falling off your bike, and your friends laughed at you? So you lied, "I wanted to do that." Are you still falling and lying about it? To whom are you lying?

You procrastinate. Projects that are completed can be scrutinized, even criticized. They open up the possibility for shame. Projects that are in a constant state of being unfinished carry a built-in excuse. There's the hope that they'll still come out perfectly as the result of some future, last-ditch effort.

You are possessive in relationships. Relationships are so difficult for you to develop and maintain that you are afraid of being deserted once you form a relationship with someone—and you hang on for dear life.

You have a high need for control. Earlier, we talked about a high level of anxiety. This condition creates a high need for control. Since your sense of well-being and security is based on externals, you're preoccupied with the status of things and the behavior of people. Every time things or people don't look or act the way you need them to, you fix, correct, adjust, improve, remedy, solve, reform, remodel or punish. This goes beyond the usual adult responsibility to guide: You need things to be "just so" in order to be able to relax. But that time never comes.

What's wrong with you? Nothing. You're *normal.* Wounded, but normal. And for someone with your relationship history, your struggles are normal, too.

In order to understand that history, let's spend some time in the next few chapters looking at some shame-based relationships. You're going to discover that a lot of your tiring traits make sense when you understand how you acquired them in the first place.

---

[3]Charles Solomon *The Ins and Outs of Rejection*, (Littleton, Colo.: Heritage House Productions, 1976), 13.

3

The Power of Past Relationships

Once there was a man who had a favorite spot by a river, a quiet, shady, wonderful place. He had just stretched out in the fragrant grass one day when he heard cries coming from the water. He spied a figure bobbing helplessly in the current. Quickly, he dived in and pulled the drowning man to the safety of the shore.

No sooner had he caught his breath than he heard another cry of distress from the river. Despite his seared lungs and aching muscles, he dived in again and rescued a second man. In fact, for the rest of that day, the man saved one person after another. When he had spent every ounce of strength, he watched in horror as many others sank to a watery doom.

Finally, in utter exhaustion, he collapsed at the water's edge and cried to the heavens, "Dear Lord, what's going on upstream?"

I learned to ask that same question early on in my work as a pastoral counselor in regard to the relationships that shape the inner views that hurting people have of themselves. You see, each of us has a relational "upstream." Friends, families, churches, teachers provide the blueprint for the way we think of ourselves and our present relationships. In turn, you and I represent the upstream for those who come after us. The treatment we have all received in past relationships is the source of a powerful current—our sense of emotional and spiritual well-being, that is, how *good* or *bad* we feel we are as human beings, and how *well* or *poorly* we think we measure up. And so the first step in turning toward the solid shore of emotional health where we can cease our inner struggling is to understand our relational upstream and how it has set the course toward our present inner state of being.

Three "Eye-Openers"

The story of the man on the riverbank illustrates my own shock and frustration as a younger man. I assumed that Christian families and good churches would be the best sources for building the emotional and spiritual health of their members. I was firmly rooted in that view when I came out of seminary and entered the ministry.

How naive I was!

Not long after I began pastoral counseling, I made three observations that blew my idealism to smithereens. Fourteen years of counseling since then have only served to confirm what I observed.

A family should be a resource that builds up and affirms the value of each member. However, my first observation was that many families actually tear down the health and self-esteem of their individual members. This can be done through overt acts, such as sexual and physical abuse. Another equally hurtful, yet less obvious, form of abuse is discounting someone's opinions and feelings, or neglecting to spend time with that person. Some will use the correct religious rhetoric about value and acceptance coming from God—but at the same time relationships in their homes actually convey messages of non-acceptance, even condemnation. Consequently, even some Christian families can be a drain on confidence and morale instead of a resource of affirmation and trust.

Secondly, I observed how a cycle, set in motion early in life, can plague and control a person long after he leaves his family of origin, infecting relationships in his future family. Some people who have been abused in turn abuse others, while others respond to their own abuse by being *passive*. Some who have been neglected in turn neglect, while others respond by being *over-involved* or smothering. In any case, *generations* of family members are affected by the original abuse. The cycle perpetuates itself: People who are hurt, hurt others.

Finally, I discovered that individuals and families are almost as shamed and exhausted from the solutions they're being given by the Christian community as they are by the problems for which they're seeking help. That's because even among Christians a focus on *appearance* often prevails. Ironically, hurting people are typically given performance-oriented solutions when their self-effort is already out of fuel. When the "formulas" fail, these folks are viewed as unspiritual for talking about their struggles and feelings—things for which they already feel bad.

To make matters worse, parents and leaders in the Christian community are sometimes held less accountable for staying healthy and honest, even though the Bible clearly indicates that those in authority are actually held *more* accountable than others. Further, those who confront parents or leaders with their inappropriate behavior are often reprimanded or labeled rebels, troublemakers.

"A Little Leaven . . ."

To grasp the power that families and churches wield, it is important to understand that both are relationship systems. The fact that they are systems gives them the ability to wound people so severely. On the positive side, it is also what makes them conducive to spreading health to their members. Scripture states the concept clearly in 1 Corinthians 5:6: "Do you not know that a little leaven leavens the whole lump?" Although this reminder was written directly to a church community, it can easily be applied to the family.

What exactly is meant when we say a family or church is a *system*? A system is simply a group of interrelated, interdependent parts. A school system, for instance, is made up of a school board, an administration, teachers, secretaries, cooks, parents, students, janitors, and transportation people among others. If the cooks stay home one day, or if the bus drivers don't show up for work, everyone else is affected.

The body of Christ is a system in that same interrelated, interdependent manner. As Paul says, "For just as the body is one and has many members, and all the members of the body, though many, are one body, so it is with Christ" (1 Cor. 12:12). Paul also says, in verse 26, "If one member suffers, all suffer together; if one member is honored, all rejoice together."

Likewise, members of families are dependent upon one another in a variety of ways. Not only that, but everything one member does, feels, or experiences affects other members in ways that are both obvious *and* subtle. Picture the family like this:

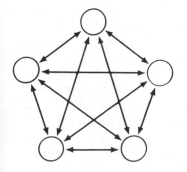

Diagram A

Each circle represents a family member. Each line represents the relationship each member has with every other member. The arrows on the end of the lines indicate that interrelatedness and interdependency which characterizes a system.

"When One Member Suffers . . ."

Paul's statement about the leaven was meant to remind the Corinthians that their whole church was weakening, because they were overlooking the immoral behavior of one member. A system will actually use more time and energy NOT dealing with issues than dealing with them. Paul also warned the Galatian Christians about the leaven of legalism (Gal. 5:9) A little leaven *will* permeate a whole lump of dough: It's not just a possibility, it's a fact. And whatever happens to one member of a church or family affects the others. Why? Because all are members of a body, a family—a system.

Systems Can Be Positive

The grip of a family system is very powerful. We are sometimes leavened in ways that are beyond our power to control or understand. I discovered this truth during an especially close yet painful time in my own family.

In 1981 my father had major surgery for cancer. Just a year later he had a relapse and was hospitalized once more. We understood that he would probably never leave the hospital this time. For some reason, I had a sense that this was my last opportunity to resolve some things between us that had been unsettled for a long time. Since I was to present a seminar in Connecticut the following week, I left my home in Minneapolis early to spend time with my dad in Madison, Wisconsin.

I spent three of the most wonderful and most *painful* days of my life with my dad less than a week before he died. Gently but directly, I was able to tell him the things he had done that hurt me. I also told him how he had helped to build and strengthen me, and I thanked him for giving me a love for the outdoors, which still serves to renew me when I'm emotionally and spiritually drained. I thanked him for his support of my ministry. Then I asked him what his favorite Bible verses were; and we talked about decisions he'd made that he would like to have made differently. I told him about the things that are important to me. We laughed together. We cried together about his impending death. My mom, grandmother, aunt and a cousin with whom I'd grown up also experienced more honesty, openness and closeness in my dad's final days than was typical of my family.

On the second afternoon of my visit, the strangest thing happened. As I got out of my car at the hospital to visit my dad, I turned to look up at his window—and a wave of nausea hit me. By that evening I was experiencing more nausea, in combination with weakness, fever, dizziness—all of my dad's symptoms.

On the morning of the third day, I could hardly get out of bed to get to the hospital. I did make it, however, and at noon I said goodbye to my dad, both of us knowing that we would not see each other again in this life.

Still experiencing his symptoms, I got into the car and headed for Connecticut. Emotionally, I was down, but the farther away I drove, the better I felt physically. Some hours later—by the time I got to Cleveland—the symptoms were gone. I'm sure there is probably a complicated psychological explanation for what happened. But to me it's very simple: "If one member suffers, all suffer together."

When the System Begins to Break Down

Dysfunctional, a term I'll use throughout the book, describes a state of not working correctly. *Dys*function is not the same as *mal*function; dysfunction carries a more serious connotation. *Malfunction* is when something works but doesn't work properly. *Dys*function is when it gets *stuck* and won't work, period. Picture a printing press with one of its minor settings off so that it prints only half a page; that's a malfunction. Now imagine that a wrench has fallen into the gears, jamming the paper and backing up the inking mechanisms— a major breakdown. The machine is stuck—dysfunctional.

A dysfunctional family has gotten stuck in unhealthy relationship patterns and actually begins breaking down its members emotionally, psychologically and spiritually. Because everyone *is* affected when one member experiences a problem, it is possible for the entire family to become unhealthy in response to the hurt, "broken," dysfunctional behavior of one member. In my book *Good News for the Chemically Dependent* (T. Nelson, 1985), I give a detailed description of how this comes about when one family member is addicted to alcohol or another mood-altering chemical. It is entirely possible for the affected family member to regain health if the family system responds in a way that's healthy. Whether healthy or unhealthy, leaven leavens.

Families don't become dysfunctional overnight; it's a process. When a family member has a personal problem, whether he shows it or not, the pain he experiences affects the others in the family.

For example—to touch upon my own story again—after my father's death in 1982, our second daughter, Erin, alternated between acting detached and being clingy. She was only five then and unable to verbalize exactly what she was feeling. She cried very easily. We were quite worried and confused because nothing we did or said seemed to help. Eventually, we talked to a counselor, and she helped us to understand some of what we were experiencing with our daughter.

You see, because of hidden hurts in my dad's past, he was often unable to cope with the behaviors of a five-year-old. He was some-times grumpy with Erin and, consequently, the two of them did not get along well. In response to his attitude, Erin wished he would go away and leave her alone. Then he died. She thought she had caused his death, and so she spilled out her pain in confused ways. Dad's dysfunctional behavior had affected her; she had been "leavened." The rest of us had been, too, in other ways.

Let's say that a problem is serious enough to physically, psycho-logically, emotionally, or spiritually cripple an individual, even *tem-porarily*. The person affected is *unable* to function effectively as a member of the system. He will contribute less to relationships and will draw more heavily on the resources of others. As a result, he will become the focus of the family's efforts as the system expends great amounts of energy seeking to function normally. It looks like this:

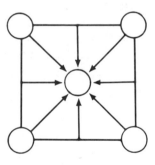

Diagram B

Notice that the family has adjusted in order to give the hurting member the attention he needs in order to recover. Note, too, the focus of energies:

What can we *do* to help?
What can we *say* so they'll get better?
Whom can we *get* them to talk to?
What books can we *read* that might help?
Whom do we *know* that could give them a job?

These and other questions, spoken and unspoken, expose the preoccupation of the family as it expends its energy to try to "fix" the wounded member.

Adjusting Is Healthy—Sometimes

Sometimes, of course, it's healthy to adjust in order to compensate for the problem a family member is experiencing. To pick up an example I've used before, let's say that a person breaks his leg—he won't be able to function as fully and efficiently as he did with two healthy legs. If all of the household jobs are to be completed, obviously someone else is going to have to do more; that is, they will have to compensate or *over*-function. This is the natural reaction of a system in an attempt to keep itself functioning and in balance.

Not only does the compensation work to keep a system operating, but it serves another healthful purpose, too. Since *under*-functioning is the means by which the leg will heal, *over*-functioning by the others buys the time necessary for the leg to heal. When the leg heals, the family readjusts back to normal, as the now-healthy family member resumes his original jobs. So, in this sense, compensation is a good thing.

Helping Mom to Be the Artist God Made Her to Be

Compensation can help the emotional and spiritual health of a family member, as well.

For example, God has created my wife, Holly, to be an artist. She acts, performs mime, directs and ministers to children through creative dramatics. Recently, she had an opportunity to audition for a part in a Christian theatrical company. We knew that if she was chosen, she would have to rehearse every night for a month and then appear in performances as booked.

As we talked about what such a step would mean to us as a family, it quickly became clear that the rest of us would have to compensate for her absence by doing more around the house. My adjustments included rearranging my speaking and counseling hours to free me up toward evenings so I'd be able to read to our little ones, see them to bed, and pray with them before lights out. There were several temporary compensations that would be necessary on the part of the kids, too. Our adjustments would enable Holly to do something her heart desired.

Holly went to the audition—and she got the part. During the time Holly was rehearsing and performing, she might have seemed, from the outside, to be "away" from the family. You might have thought this diagram was an accurate description of our family:

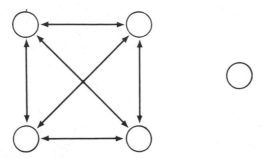

Diagram C

Actually, during that time the family looked more like Diagram B. Holly was the focus of our family. Much of what we did was a direct result of our relationship with her. Our *over*-functioning as family members allowed her to *under*-function as a family member. And at the end of the play our family dynamics readjusted to resemble Diagram A once again. If you talk to a family who has had a runaway child, you will find that even though that child was geographically absent, they were still in the center of the family. Because families *are* systems, there really can never be a Diagram C.

When Adjusting Is Unhealthy

Our hope is that God will use Holly to point people to himself, and that being able to use her talents for Him will confirm His call on her life.

Let's suppose, however, that Holly decides she wants to perform in plays all the time. Performing meets so many of her needs and she feels so useful to God that she concludes He is calling her to perform even at the expense of the family. The kids would probably feel sad and scared about this. (I know it would scare me.) I'd like to think that we'd be sharp enough to catch this imbalance and confront it.

But the truth might be different: Because we're a family that cares about our mom's self-esteem, and because we want to encourage each other to follow where God is leading, we would probably have a hard time disagreeing at first. After all, Mom would be so happy, and so many people would be touched by her acting. And how can you argue with "God's will"?

If we didn't confront the problem, some of the adjustments we made on a temporary basis would have to become more permanent.

Holly's jobs would become our jobs. It would no longer be as it was when we joyfully did more so she could do less. Now, we would *have* to over-perform to keep our family functioning as close to normal as possible. But who would function as the mom if she weren't around? Me? One of the kids?

We would have to adjust emotionally, too. To focus on the kids: Would they be sad? Sure they would. And what if they were punished or termed "unspiritual" for being sad, instead of being encouraged to tell Mom how they really felt? What if they learned to hide their hurt and loneliness because they were made to feel that God needed their mom more than they did? (I hope you see that tossing "God's will" into the mix doesn't make the situation right; it just makes it harder to confront.) What if they were made to cover up for Mom and justify her absence when friends asked why she wasn't around anymore?

Families That Are *Stuck*

There is a bottom line to all of this. Compensation or over-functioning by family members enables one to under-function when he needs to do so. But it can also enable a member to under-function just because he *chooses* to do so. And if this is done with little regard to the impact on others, it helps that member become irresponsible. And the better the system over-compensates for that member, the less accountable to the family he has to be. The system might become so expert at over-compensating that it becomes dysfunctional—that is, stuck in the broken position.

Once a family has become stuck in unhealthy roles, the irresponsible member *does not have to resume his place in the family*. He is allowed, by the dynamics of the family relationships, to remain irresponsible even though other family members would say that they desperately want him back and functioning normally again. There might even come a day when the long-lost member wants to re-enter the family as a contributing member. On this day, they will have great difficulty allowing him to do so, because the system has become so expert at functioning without his contributions. At this point, the family actually does not *need* him anymore.

The Power of Relationships

Relationships teach us about right and wrong, and about reality. For instance, some women who discover their husbands are having affairs (especially those women whose dads cheated on their moms) actually believe that their husbands cheat on them because they deserve it. That is, until a counselor or caring friend breaks the bubble of unreality by insisting that adultery and deception are never justifiable. In this way, relationships also help us learn about God, life and ourselves. They inscribe in us messages about who we are, why we're here and what we're worth.

Because of the power of relationships, many have even come to believe that even their perceptions of life are wrong and off-base. That's why a woman can get to the point of saying, "I thought *I* was wrong to let his affair *matter* so much. After all, he's really a good man, shouldn't I just respond by accepting it?" But it matters a great deal if you have come from relationship systems (family or church) that have inscribed in you a sense of worthlessness. It matters a lot if you've been taught to work for what should be gifts—love and acceptance—and to be ashamed of who you are because you never seem to be "good enough."

Now is the time for you to take shame and all its ramifications in your life seriously—to unlearn all the wrong responses you were taught.

The initial step in any healing process is to get the full picture of the illness, and this is also true when it comes to undoing the effects of shame. In the next chapter, I'm going to explain in further detail how we come to be victims of shame. I'll illustrate more clearly the dynamics of shame-based relationships—that is, relationships that inscribe in you a sense of worthlessness or defectiveness instead of worth and wholeness.

I am confident that once you understand the all-pervading nature of shame's leaven and the power of shame-based systems, you will also begin to understand the importance of rebuilding relationship systems so that they communicate love, acceptance and grace.

4

When Shame Is the Name of the Game

Mary's mother was ill and was expected to die.

As Mary and I talked in my church office one afternoon, she told me the painful story of how their relationship had broken down long ago. Mary's mother was an impeccably groomed, always punctual and precise perfectionist who had virtually driven her daughter away from her through repeated embarrassments. They hadn't even spoken much for the past fifteen years. Now, a phone call alerted Mary that her mother was flying in from another city for a visit, undoubtedly her last. "This is my big chance to reconcile with her," Mary said, wringing her hands. "But I'm all torn up inside. I'm confused. Nervous. Excited. *Terrified.* What if she won't listen? What if she won't forgive me? What if I *can't* forgive her?"

Mary's lifestyle was pretty laid back. Her house was small and modestly decorated. She dressed unpretentiously. But Mother was coming! Time to do something special. Since Mom was going to be there for three days, Mary had gone out and bought three bright new dresses. She'd had a friend come over to help her perk up the house with fresh wall paint and new curtains. As Mary left my office, she was a nervous wreck.

When Mary came in for her next counseling session, her mother had come and gone and she gave me a glowing report: "Mom and I got along great. We said what we needed to say to each other. I feel like we're reconciled."

Then in the next breath, Mary broke into tears. I was confused by the contradiction. When she'd composed herself a little, I asked, "Why are you crying?"

She replied, "I *still* don't know if my mom loves and accepts me.

I didn't show her the real me. She saw clothes and decorations I don't usually have. She liked those. But would she have been the same if I hadn't gone through all the external stuff? Would she have liked *me*?"

Mary had done everything "right"; she had lived up to her mother's standard (whether real or imagined) and still come out feeling unloved and unaccepted. What prevented Mary from feeling affirmed? I think the answer lies both in what happened and in what *didn't* happen in Mary's life. What *did* happen was that the wounding, shaming messages that were deeply ingrained in Mary's heart were not erased by one positive visit. In addition, some essential and non-negotiable needs *were not* met. Now, she was experiencing the real message of the visit: "You're acceptable and good only because you've lived up to my standards."

In Mary's case, she had been subjected to years of critical remarks long before she left home, followed by years of almost no contact because she failed to measure up. Not everyone has to experience such an exaggerated rejection in order to develop a shame-based identity. In fact, what might be an insignificant remark or action to one person can be devastating to another. Many factors come into play—including expectations, sensitivity and even the context in which the rejection occurs.

Jane, one of my former clients, is a very fine artist. During one session, she remembered a painful event that occurred almost sixteen years before.

At fourteen, she had painted a picture and entered it in the county fair competition. Even though she was competing with many skilled adults, the judges awarded her the blue ribbon. When she brought the ribbon and picture home, her parents threw a party and invited family and friends. While the celebration was going on, however, her dad took her aside and, pointing to an object in the picture, said, "This is really a fine picture, Jane—but wouldn't it have been better if this were in a different spot?"

Through tears, she told me that when her father made that comment, she thought, *I'm finished with that picture. In fact, I'm sure the judges think I'm finished, too. But I guess I could have done better.*

Remembering that event triggered a lot of other memories for Jane about the messages she received in her family. All of them said that not only was she incapable of doing something good enough, she was incapable of *knowing* if something was good enough. This had devastating effects on her sensitive and naturally perceptive nature.

What Is a "Shame-Based" System?

As we've already touched upon, a shame-based system can be a family, church or group in which an individual is given the message that he is defective and inadequate as a human being; eventually, he becomes ingrained with a deep sense of "dysgrace."[1]

By God's design, the primary channel for learning one's identity, for having needs met, for understanding who God is, and for developing relationships is the family.[2] In order to prevent shame from being passed through us to future generations, we must recognize the shame-producing characteristics of unhealthy relationship systems. The following is a list of ten characteristics that best describe the relationship systems, past and/or present, under which tired, wounded people labor:

1. "Out-loud" shaming

While all shame-based systems shame people, the first is the only one that refers to overt shaming: *"Out-loud"* shaming.

Comparing one person to another causes shame. Name-calling causes shame. Phrases like "What's wrong with you?" and "What an idiot you are!" will shame a person. So does raising the standard after a task is completed, saying, "Well, you did *that* well enough—but you *didn't* do. . . ." You don't measure up!

The following characteristics will show how shame is transmitted in silent or more subtle ways. And because the shaming occurs covertly, it is often harder to confront, untangle and overcome.

2. Shame-based systems are performance-oriented

We all need an environment where we feel our needs are met because of who we are and not because of what we do.[3] In shame-based relationships, value and acceptance are earned on the basis of performance. Performance, however, always seems to fall short of the standard, giving us the message, "You are defective and inadequate." Eventually, we become ingrained with a need to measure up. What follows is more impotent performance, which generates even more shame. And on it goes.

Unfortunately, we can also see this pattern in the relationship

---

[1]David Seamands, *Healing Grace* (Victor Books, 1988), 39.
[2]Lynn Heitritter & Jeanette Vought, *Helping Victims of Sexual Abuse* (Minneapolis: Bethany House, 1989), 61.
[3]David Seamands, *Healing Grace*, 94.

many Christians have with God. Never before have there been so many "how-to" seminars and books (on everything from prayer to potty training, it seems!) in which Christians are told they will find the "key" to closeness with God. And never before have so many spiritually tired Christians been wounded and in need of counseling.

Trying hard is not the solution. When someone becomes a Christian, he has a brand new identity as a child of God because of the cross of Christ. But the truth is, people are affirmed in our society, in families and even in our churches for what they *do,* not for who they *are.* When a person comes into a relationship with Christ, most of the teaching he receives is about how Christians are supposed to act, not who a Christian *is* as a new creation in Christ.

Likewise, most parents get a sense of value from the performance of their kids, and husbands and wives draw a sense of value from the capabilities, career and attentiveness of their spouses. "Be good Christian husbands, wives, parents and kids!"

What *is* it that makes us acceptable, valuable people? We're often taught that acceptability comes from "useful" religious performance that lives up to the expectations of our particular religious community. And since human performance is an inadequate, false means to acquire value, it *always* falls short. Someone is always displeased, and even if *he* isn't dissatisfied, *we* are. We simply can't act perfectly enough.

3. Unspoken rules govern shame-based systems

The rules that reign supreme in shame-based relationships are seldom, if ever, spoken out loud. In fact, the only time you can be sure that an unspoken rule is there is if you break it. Two specific unspoken rules that are more damaging than any others are these: "Can't talk," and "Can't win."

The "Can't-talk" rule is easy to understand. It goes something like this: "There really aren't any problems here. If you think there is a problem, *you* are the problem." The truth of the matter is that some parents (in a family system) and some pastors (in a church system) are threatened, afraid of what the existence of a problem "says" about them as human beings and leaders. In other words, if there is a problem—or even a *question*—then the person raising the issue must be challenging them. No matter how gently the question is raised (when the question is raised at all), *you* become the issue in a shame-based system. It's as if naming a problem out loud *caused* the problem to exist, which, of course, is not true. Individuals in this kind of system learn not to bring up a problem or question for fear of making waves.

The "Can't-talk" rule is a given in shame-based relationships for three reasons. First, if my value and acceptance are earned by my performance, then any lapse in performance shames me and *can't* be talked about. Secondly, if a lapse in my performance cannot be covered up, then I must project the blame away from myself so I can avoid being shamed. Therefore, if you confront me, I'll blame you for making a big deal out of nothing, or for being oversensitive.

Francine's story illustrates how this works. Francine was being physically abused by her husband. Through the encouragement of friends she decided to report the abuse to authorities. Her husband was arrested and put in jail.

I might ask, "Why did Francine's husband go to jail?" and many people might answer, "Because Francine called the police!" The truth is, he went to jail because he abused Francine. He broke the law. Beating your wife is illegal in all fifty states. However, the message given to Francine by her husband and echoed by his family and even their pastor was: "You are disloyal, unforgiving and unsubmissive. You overreacted!" The unspoken message was: "Being beaten by someone is not the problem; the problem is that *you* weren't strong enough to take a few slaps, punches and kicks without crying like a baby." When victims believe that message, they don't call the police. And when they don't call the police, the abuse continues. But the truth is, it was perfectly right for Francine to hold her husband accountable for his behavior.

The "Can't-talk" rule has yet a third function. In order for all of the unspoken rules to have power to control people's lives, they must *remain* unspoken. "Can't talk" keeps them that way.

The "Can't-win" rule is really two contradictory rules combined into one. Here are just a few examples:

> "Always tell the truth; but, when we go to Grandma's, don't tell her you hate her bread stuffing. If she asks, just be polite, eat it and say you like it."
>
> "Honesty is the best policy; but, if so-and-so calls, tell them I'm not here."
>
> "Don't keep anything from your parents; but, Mother (or Father) would be so upset if they knew this, so please don't tell them."

The problem is that if a person acts on one rule, he is shamed for failing at the other. No performance is good enough, and since performance is the issue, shame is the result.

Here are some other examples of unspoken rules that govern shame-based systems. Unless recognized and purposefully rejected, members of the system will apply them in their future relationships without even being aware of it.

"What's *real* doesn't matter; how things *look* is what matters."

"What other people think is most important."

"Adults are more important than children."

"Adults always know what children need, feel, and want better than children."

"People who feel sad are oversensitive."

"Something is wrong with people who feel at all."

"Feelings don't matter."

"Certain feelings are wrong."

"Not showing feelings is the same as not having them."

"If parents are upset, the behavior of their kids is the cause."

"If parents are upset, the behavior of the kids is the solution."

"It's okay for parents to act inappropriately in order to get their kids to act appropriately."

"There's a different set of ethical and moral rules for adults than there is for kids."

"It's better to be seen and not heard."

"Kids have to act fifteen years older than they really are."

"If you can't say something nice, don't say anything at all."

"We can solve all of our problems ourselves."

"We don't have any problems."

"Questioning is disrespectful."

"It's never okay to say *no* to an adult."

"Women are here to do what men want."

"There's a different set of rules for men than there is for women."

"When men are upset you'd better take them seriously. When women are upset it must be their 'time of the month,' or they're just being oversensitive. (You know how women are)."

"God helps those who help themselves."

"Peace at all costs."

"It's not okay to have needs—needs are selfish."

The list goes on and on. While they remain unspoken they have power to control. When they are said out loud, they look as inappropriate and shaming as they are.

Some of you reading the above list may have begun to feel "guilty" for letting yourself admit that your families actually treated you that way. Actually, it isn't guilt. The "Can't-talk" rule shames anyone who brings the unspoken rules into the light. Left in the dark, the rules have an incredible amount of power.

One last thought on the power of unwritten rules—in a shame-based system, these rules have more power than written ones. For example, the Bible says in Ephesians 4:25, "Therefore, putting away falsehood, let every one speak the truth with his neighbor. . . ." The *written* rule, then, is "Be honest." The *unwritten* rule is "Be nice." Even in families and churches that profess to care *a lot* about what the Bible says, many times the unwritten rule prevails. Which rule won in your family?

4. People in shame-based systems "code" when they talk

Growing up with "Can't-talk," "Can't-win" and other unspoken rules creates the need to code what you say.

For instance, many people I've talked with were raised with an unspoken rule that says, "Favors aren't optional." That means when Mom or Dad said, "Would you do me a favor?" they meant, "Do it!" You didn't have the option to say no. It wasn't a favor, after all; it was a command, but it sounded "nicer" to call it a favor. However, a "non-optional favor" is confusing; it's a contradiction. Parents say no to your favors, right? On top of that, if you noticed the unspoken rule and said it out loud ("It seems as if favors aren't optional in this family," or "It feels as if adults are more important than kids"), then *you* were shamed for being "disrespectful" to adults. *You* became the problem.

It very swiftly becomes clear that needs, honest feelings, questions and opinions that differ are not okay. Therefore, people have to learn to get what they need or let out what's inside by putting it in code. Saying things straight gets you labeled as the problem.

In shame-based families and churches, members have invisible code books that they carry in their heads, though most of them are unaware they are doing so. The code book is an absolute essential if you are to survive in a shame-based system. It helps you to code things you want to say to others with the least amount of waves possible. It helps you to understand what others are saying so you can use the necessary, shame-avoiding behavior. It teaches you very unhealthy communication patterns. And it keeps people apart. Let me show you how this works.

My dad collected HO-scale electric trains. One day during a visit to his house, he and I were having a conversation on the sofa downstairs. From the upstairs bedroom we heard Erin, who was then three, playing with a bellows train whistle. One of the ways my dad coded was to "talk to the air." It was an unintentional habit. When he heard the sound of his whistle, he looked off in the distance and said, "Yup, that's a forty-dollar whistle. Hope she doesn't break it."

Having grown up with my dad's code, I knew what to do. I had my code book section on "Decoding Air Talk" memorized. I knew that what he *really* meant to say was, "Go get my expensive whistle away from your daughter."

How about this one: "It sure would be nice if somebody around here would take out the garbage." Read your code book—that really means, "You're supposed to do it." What if you ignore the code? "Boy, I can't get any of these lazy people around here to take out the garbage." Read your code book—that means, "Shame on you. You're supposed to take out the garbage." What's a good enough reason to take out the garbage? Because it's *full*! In shame-based families people take out the garbage to protect themselves from being shamed, or in response to the hot poker-like message that we are lazy creatures if we don't.

Was my father unreasonable for wanting to make sure his whistle didn't get broken? No. Was he incapable of protecting his own whistle? No. Was my daughter so ferocious that he would have gotten hurt if he tried to approach her? No. Was it my job to get in the middle of their relationship and make it turn out all right? No! Who was responsible for the relationship between my father and my daughter? For people to be close, they need to have direct relationships with each other, not through someone else. Many people expend a lot of energy propping up weak relationships, trying to make everyone believe they're good ones.

Triangling. This brings me to another unhealthy aspect about coding—called "triangling." Triangular relationships are an issue in almost every family I counsel. Dad wants child to clean out the garage. Dad tells Mom. Mom codes it to make it "less hurtful." She tells child, "It would be nice if you'd clean out the garage." Child ignores the coded message, or promises to do it later. Mom codes the child's response to make it more palatable. She tells Dad, "He misunderstood—don't be upset." Who do you think gets tired in this triangle?

Not long after my father died, I looked at my mom one day and realized that I didn't know her very well. Various things contributed to this, but one of them was the fact that the focus of our relationship all too often was my father. Much of the energy in our relationship was spent on decoding messages and trying not to upset Dad. But now the focal point of our relationship for twenty-nine years, my dad, was gone. Consequently, the relationship between my mother and me suddenly looked as neglected as it truly was.

5. Shame-based families are idolatrous

To suggest that families, especially Christian ones, could be idolatrous may strike you as a pretty harsh judgment. You may envision golden calves, fat clay statues, or scantily clad men and women dancing around a sacred yucca plant. But idolatry, as I've said earlier, simply means turning to a source other than God to meet your needs.

Remember the "Can't-win" rule and Grandma's bread stuffing? If telling Grandma that you'd prefer not to eat her stuffing ruins her holiday and she feels like a less-special human being, then the truth is, she's getting a measure of her value and identity from her cooking and people's opinion of it. What a poor source of value! This is also a form of idolatry, because the true source of our worth and identity is God. If you help Grandma to keep this false source of value at the expense of your honesty, then you actually encourage her to remain touchy and immature. You will continue to feel a lack of closeness toward her, and you'll continue to dread going to her house. You're protecting, at the expense of your integrity (not to mention your taste buds), an illusion of peace and closeness that doesn't really exist at all. This is not a relationship; it is an arrangement. True, there are kind and tactful ways of saying things—but don't mistake lying for "being nice."

Grandma really won't benefit from her family's tiptoeing around her false gods. She needs to know that she is a loved, accepted person, even when the stuffing doesn't turn out right. You can say, "No thank you. I don't want any stuffing. But I love *you,* Grandma!" How much more honest and graceful that is than to be dishonest to Grandma while looking for more and more "nice" excuses not to visit next time.

6. Shame-based systems have a hard time with kids

Since the rules that govern these systems are mostly unspoken, it's almost impossible to live up to the standard. You never know where you stand. Needs, feelings, opinions, a certain behavior (and even the opposite behavior)—*everything* has the potential to bring on a sense of shame—especially to kids.

Everything must be perfect; so-and-so is coming. Watch what you say, because so-and-so gets upset easily. You must walk on eggs, take everything very seriously, watch your *P*'s and *Q*'s, tow the line, get your ducks lined up, and act your age (which means much older than you are). Don't laugh too hard at jokes. Don't make too much noise or have too much fun when you're playing. Don't talk at the table. And never, *never* run in church.

It's not okay for kids to be kids in shame-based families or churches. They must be miniature adults. But healthy kids are constantly in the process of finding out what's real. It's the job of children to experiment with life. It's an imperfect, even messy process. Consequently, kids in a shame-based system get shamed a lot.

7. Shame-based systems are preoccupied with fault and blame

People make choices. Some are wise, others are unwise. Some are right, others are wrong. It's okay to hold people responsible or accountable for their actions. But shame-based systems don't merely hold people accountable for their choices. They *indict* people on the basis of behaviors. *Fault* and *blame* are the issues, not responsibility.

Behaviors have an awful lot of power in these systems. *Too much power*. This can be seen in the way a lapse in performance is handled. If someone else's performance—or a behavior, a choice, an appearance—has the power to make a statement about me, I have to make sure that blame is concretely fixed on them in order to push that shame away from me.

Let's say that a church invites a guest speaker to preach on a Sunday morning. Unfortunately, to everyone's dismay, the speaker uses some crude expressions and makes several statements that are out-and-out heresy.

In a shame-based church, the follow-up to such an event would be this: The congregation would criticize and blame the pastor and elders for inviting the speaker; the pastor and elders would, in turn, assign specific blame to the person who recommended the speaker, in order to prove to the congregation the mistake was not their "fault." All this activity, rather than simply saying, "Sorry folks. Guess we'll never have *that* speaker back here!"

In short, shame-based systems burn up a lot of energy in self-defense, and in asking, "Who's responsible?" And the question isn't raised for the purpose of helping the guilty party face the consequences—much less so that forgiveness can be extended. It is raised because we need to know whom we should shame, or who should be made to feel bad. After all, if we can make people feel bad enough about their behaviors, they'll stop, right?

Shame-based systems *overreact* to the choices of their members. You can never perform well enough, and you can never be sorry enough when you don't perform. When a mistake is made, people in this system need to say they are sorry (whether they are sorry or not). But when they say they're sorry, they get the message, "Sorry isn't good enough." There is no way of doing it right, of saying you're sorry, or of correcting the mistake—no way to escape being shamed.

8. Shame-based systems are strong on "head skills"

People in shame-based relationships live basically in a defensive mode. Shame hurts. It cuts to the heart. Therefore, people must become experts at "self-defense" techniques to protect themselves against shaming messages. These include: denying the existence of problems or rationalizing them away, blaming others and becoming a good debater.

In shame-based systems people are constantly interrogated. But the questions asked have no answers. "I just can't understand why you did that! Is your head on backwards?" "Whatever possessed you to say that?" "Why did you do that?" The only safe answer is "I don't know." Any other answer would be analyzed and made to look foolish.

9. Shame-based systems are weak on "heart skills"

The only feelings allowed in a shame-based system are those which can be justified or understood. Emotions must be *thought,* not *felt.* If you can't explain the feeling, then it must not exist. Experiencing or expressing certain emotions such as sadness, hurt, loneliness, or humiliation is viewed as an indication of weakness or defectiveness. All efforts by members of the system to fix or change those feelings only shame a person for feeling that way and "causing" so much upset.

People in shame-based relationships think that if they can understand *why* they feel the way they do, then the feeling will go away. Moreover, they believe that feelings *should* go away. Consequently, they get stuck carrying a lot of heavy emotions and are never able to resolve them.

Compliments, compassion and empathy are reserved for those outside the system. Janet's story illustrates this point. When Janet brought friends home, her parents showed real interest in their hobbies, interests, grades and accomplishments. Compliments flowed.

But Janet's performance was criticized or ignored. Other times her parents would brag about her to others, while she distinctly felt that the bragging was only to gain a sense of worth for themselves. She did the hard work, but never got the compliments. Her parents' rationale was, "We don't want you to get a big head." Well, it worked!

10. *People in shame-based systems only* look *as if their needs are met*

People come away from shame-based systems with a sense that they are:

- *Not* loved and accepted (not even lovable or acceptable)
- *Only* loved and accepted if, when, or because they perform
- *Not* capable, valuable, or worthwhile
- *Very* alone, not really belonging anywhere, to anything, or with anyone

Finally, the shame-based family or church is a system that is *upside-down*. A shame-based relationship system isn't there to pour strength and fullness into its members. Instead, it draws *from* its members in order to perpetuate itself. The members are so needy, however, that they are not capable of filling anyone else's needs. This leaves the members and the system still in need, and *everyone* indicted for failing. The shame and neediness in the system passes on to the members, to future relational systems, and to subsequent generations. But since love and acceptance are something to be earned, members have learned to be good performers. They've had to. The result is the person I think David Seamands is talking about when he describes the "Superself": empty and disconnected on the inside with the appearance of fullness on the outside.[4]

The problem with shame—whether it's passed on in silence or with loud shouting—is that it's crippling. In fact, it's like a living death: You spend your life feeling as though you're not good enough, living according to performance, never measuring up, and *always wondering when you're going to start living and being happy*.

The reason so many people do not feel fully alive, or that part of them is dead inside, is that they have not been fully awakened to life. But life is here to be had and enjoyed freely.

I want to show you now how you can choose not to listen to those "killing" voices—how to choose *life*!

---

[4]David Seamands, *Healing Grace*, 99.

5

Run Over by Shame

"How ya doin', fat face?"

Not a very flattering comment, to say the least. What would your response be if someone said that to you? Would you feel hurt? Probably. Would you ignore or avoid the person who made the comment? Perhaps. Would you lash out at that person? Hopefully not. Would you confront the other person with his hurtful behavior? Hopefully.

Would you feel like committing suicide? Though that may sound extreme, you might even consider suicide, depending on your inner state when the remark was made.

Recently, I read about the tragedy of a family in a town not far from my home in Minneapolis. Anita, the family's teenage daughter, had committed suicide, and it came as a complete shock to those who knew and loved her. Bewildered friends said it seemed totally "out of character." Anita had so many things going for her. She was a senior in high school, an honor student, a cheerleader, president of this and captain of that. Her suicide made no sense.

Then some other pieces of the puzzle were revealed. Sure, she had some major bouts with depression. And there was that time when she withdrew from family and friends. And she did have a history of struggling with anorexia nervosa (the eating disorder characterized by self-starvation). Her family seemed to quickly dismiss all this as "in the past." Anita had been in extensive therapy, but after that "brief, dark period in her life" she rebounded. She out-performed everyone's expectations. No one expected *this*.

As we've already seen, relationships have a lot of power to communicate shaming messages to people. The truth is, Anita's choice was just the end of a long process set in motion by a comment that made her feel like a defective human being: Someone had called her "fat." As Anita processed the comment in her mind, it took on other

51

meanings that, most likely, were never intended by the person who'd made the comment. She believed the gross lie that "thin" is the only standard of perfect beauty; that to be a few pounds overweight means you are unacceptable; and that she was, therefore, defective. That was how Anita processed the stray and foolish comment that made her feel ashamed.

All processes have beginnings. Some begin at birth and are fueled by shaming messages received in the context of shame-based relationships. However, shaming messages can come from many sources, not always from long-term relationships. They can be communicated by daily events: an accident, a poor choice, a bad grade, a circumstance, a look . . . a comment.

I'm accustomed to hearing clients' stories about traumatic events they've experienced. In addition to whatever hurtful feelings they may have felt, there's often a great sense of personal indictment for having had the experience at all. Throughout the rest of this chapter, I'll describe some of the other sources that wound and shame people. I won't offer a thorough examination of each type of event, because other books have been written dealing with each of them in great detail. My goal is simply to show the link between people's shame and certain events they experience: "bad" behavior, divorce, abuse, addiction, and so forth. To help you see the relationship between an event and the feeling of defectiveness, I'll present what I believe is the real *meaning* of the event, and then describe how a shaming *message* is communicated.

Personal Behavior

The meaning. People make choices for which they are ultimately responsible. In this world's culture, behavior that violates established social and moral standards is called an infraction of the law—a misdemeanor or a felony. In social settings, actions that don't conform to what is generally expected are called breaches of etiquette, or bad taste. In God's economy, a choice, attitude or motive that fails to live up to His standard is called a sin. In fact, the Greek word used for sin, *hamartia*, means falling short, or missing the mark. When we miss the mark—whether with God, family, friends; in public, or within ourselves—we are dealing with *behaviors,* not our *value* and *acceptance* as a human being.

The message. People in various areas of society, as well as many families and churches, fail to separate people from their behaviors.

Through our efforts to confront, correct or control the actions of others, we send messages that say defective behaviors indicate personal defectiveness. "Hate the sin, but love the sinner" is a good idea—but one that is not very often lived out.

In systems that are performance-oriented, missing the mark *always* brings on shame. An offhanded comment, a flare-up of anger, an accident, a divorce, having an abortion—all have the power to indict. Consequently, the transgressor will carry shame for behaviors long since past, whether or not they can be categorized as sin. In a society or circle where any unacceptable behavior is shamed, the offender becomes an expert at heaping shame upon himself. In the final analysis, no one else even needs to add to it—he is already self-condemned.

Divorce

The meaning. Divorce is about people's behaviors and choices. It's a traumatic experience for everyone involved. When two people get divorced it's usually the end of a long process of relationship breakdown. Ask most divorced people and they'll tell you the real divorce happened long before the date on which they signed the divorce papers. The document just acknowledged the breakdown, the inability or unwillingness of the individuals to resolve the painful issues, and it notarized their willingness to make all of that public.

The message. For many people, divorce is more painful than the death of a loved one because it signals intentional rejection. A tearful client told me recently, "It wouldn't have hurt as much if he had died." It also brings to the surface much of the shame that's already there as the result of living in a dysfunctional family system.

Many times, the parents of a divorced couple will interpret the divorce as an indictment against them as parents.

Likewise, children of divorce often feel they are to blame for the failure of their parents' marriage. These kids have probably been trying to put Band-Aids on their folks' marital pain for a long time, lying to others, not inviting friends over, trying to be "good," or finding ways to disappear. The lack of improvement in the marriage makes them feel defective—as if they somehow should have been "adequate" to fix a breakdown between two adults. Since they interpret all of their own attempts to "try harder" as *love* for their parents, their parents' refusal to try harder translates into a message like this: "Even though you love us enough to make our marriage work, we don't love you enough to make it work"; or "Nice try, kids, but you didn't do the right things to save our marriage." Because children normally see things from a self-centered viewpoint, they do in fact "receive" messages of defectiveness like this—even when they are never intended.

For the divorced adult, his or her inability to resolve problems also translates into personal "defectiveness." "What's wrong with me that I couldn't work this out? How could I have picked this person in the first place? I should have listened to so-and-so. What will people think of me?" This is compounded when one spouse wants to reconcile and the other doesn't.

In addition, other people, churches and society in general contribute to the shame already there with attitudes and comments that insinuate that divorce makes you less of a man, a woman, or a Christian. A comment I hear quite often from divorced clients is this: "I'd feel more accepted in church if I'd *murdered* someone."

In cases where a spouse has had an extramarital affair, their mate is left with the message that there's something wrong with them and that's why they have been replaced. Most will never see their spouse's affair simply for what it is: an immoral choice made by another person. Often, they go to great lengths to improve themselves in order to win back their spouse. They set up walls against future relationships to prevent further hurt and shame. Sometimes they rush to replace their lost spouse with another relationship in an attempt to drown out the voice that says, "Something's wrong with *you*." That voice comes through even more loud and clear if their spouse decides to leave them and remarry. And where children are involved, desertion by a parent can be more difficult than losing him or her through death.[1]

Addiction

The meaning. Addiction is simply the end of a course of action designed to fill inner spiritual emptiness with something that can't fill it. It is the result of an attempt to meet inner needs with external substances or activities. People can become addicted to many things. If a person believes that money, work, food, diet, chemicals, exercise, a relationship, or a ministry has the power to meet his needs and make him a more valuable, acceptable person, he will set out on whatever course is required to obtain it. He may pay dearly in other

---

[1]Gary Smalley and John Trent, *The Blessing* (Nashville: Thomas Nelson, Inc., 1986), 141.

areas of his life to have it. He might sacrifice money, sleep, meals, integrity, or time with others in order to possess a given object or attain a given goal.

In addition, once he's invested so much of his life's energy in the pursuit of such an object or goal, it becomes easier to continue investing than to let go of what's already been invested. And once he possesses what he sought, he's not likely to let it go without a fight.[2]

The message. Addiction devastates relationships. The addictive course of action consumes most or all of the addict's emotions, effort and energy; therefore, others suffer neglect. Regardless of what words are spoken, what is communicated to those who care about the addicted person is this: "You are not important. My addiction is not negotiable; you and your well-being *are*. It's okay for me to take you for granted."

The "Can't-talk" rule is the primary mode of operation where there is addiction. When a person attempts to meet his needs through a "negative" addiction (alcohol, drugs, sex, food, gambling), family and friends are shamed for taking notice. The fact that there *is* an addiction is so shaming that anyone who notices the problem or confronts it out loud becomes the problem. And when a person tries to meet his needs through a "positive" addiction (work, ministry, a "friendship"), those trying to help are shamed for questioning because the course being pursued here is, on the surface, desirable and "acceptable." The one who confronts this kind of problem is treated as petty, unreasonable, unspiritual, oversensitive, jealous, selfish or critical.

Additionally, people affected by someone else's addiction react psycho-emotionally, by learning to adjust their thoughts and feelings in order to make sense out of a painful situation. In other words, they learn to pretend not to notice what they see, think what they think, or feel what they feel. Functionally, people react by learning to contribute more, compensating for the fact that the addicted person is contributing less. Both reactions are an attempt to overcome, undo, or at least cope with the presence of the addiction.

Unfortunately, these reactions actually help perpetuate the addiction. Therefore, a sense of failure and shame transfers to those who would like to help. Usually, they try harder. At some point, it becomes easier for them to continue investing more emotion and energy to "recover" their loved one than to let go of what they've already in-

---

[2]For a more complete examination of addiction, and its effects upon relationships; how to help the addicted and their loved ones, see my book *Good News for the Chemically Dependent*, (T. Nelson, 1985).

vested. Admitting to a lack of control, or admitting you can't recover someone alone, is equated with an admission of some inner defect. The one who would help is now in his own addictive process, believing that a certain course of action (their efforts) can fill their inner emptiness (shame).

Abusiveness

The meaning. Like the other issues discussed already, abuse is a complex subject. What further complicates it is the fact that there are so many forms of abuse. There is sexual abuse—incest, rape, sexual molestation and other violations of a person's sexuality. There is violent abuse—physical injury to spouse, children, or the aged. And there is psycho-emotional abuse—verbal abuse or neglect.

One great obstacle to recognizing and combatting abuse is the lack of a clear definition. What *is* abuse? When is behavior toward someone abusive? Abuse, in my definition, is when Person A uses his power or his position and authority to force Person B to perform in order to meet the needs of Person A. Most people define abuse only as hitting or molesting. They overlook all of the subtle and sometimes more damaging forms of abuse. By my definition, when a parent uses his or her authority or power solely to control a child to act in a way that meets the inner need of the parent, *it is abuse*. It is abuse whether they control through the use of violence, a loud voice, threats, manipulation, or Bible verses.

For example: I may want everyone in my church to respect me as a good Christian father. But at a church picnic my kids get tired and whiney. Many Christian parents feel that a child should never show his tiredness by complaining, but always be perfectly polite in front of other adults. (In other words, be more "perfect" than they are themselves!) If my self-esteem and respect from others is threatened by my children's "misbehavior," then I'll be more concerned about knocking them into line than I am concerned about their physical need for quiet and rest. I may even belittle them in front of others, or lecture them from the Scriptures. This is putting my needs before theirs. This is abuse.

There are several issues at work within the perpetrator of abuse: his own shame; his unmet needs; his lack of appropriate skills in meeting his needs; and his struggle to seek some external means— the performance or behavior of someone else—to erase or temporarily forget his own inner sense of defectiveness. The flaw in this method is that no one's shame can be eradicated by the performance of another. The sense of being flawed is further compounded by the fact that once the incident of abuse is over, the abuser experiences even more shame.

Violent sexual abuse is an external expression of the offender's inner shame and rage and desire to punish. The sexual organ is simply the weapon of choice. Incest is the attempt of the offender to meet his unmet need for love, acceptance and intimacy with a person who is less able or willing to reject him than others have been. Sex is simply the means. Covert forms of sexual abuse (exhibitionism, voyeurism) represent still "safer" ways for offenders to attempt to meet needs or act out inner pain. Again, sex is simply the method.

Violent physical abuse is the extreme attempt to control another person. It's so important to an offender that another person act in a certain way that he controls that other person's actions by inflicting harm. Control is the main issue for these abusers: They attempt to control another, while neglecting to control themselves. In addition to physical battering, other extremely damaging abuse occurs when the abuser acts violently toward pets or the possessions of the victim. Sexual activity against the victim's will, battering during the sex act, and forcing someone to perform sexually in a way that's humiliating are other forms of abuse.

Psycho-emotional abuse is, in some ways, more damaging than physical abuse. Black eyes are at least a tangible evidence that abuse has occurred. Wounds to the heart are deeper and invisible to others. Again, the attempt to control another seems to be the main issue in this type of abuse. Verbal abuse, the most easily recognized form of psycho-emotional abuse, includes name-calling, put-downs, comparing to others, raising the voice and threats.

There are other more subtle forms of abuse, including: drawing the attention of others to a person's mistakes in order to humiliate him; threatening violence; threatening suicide; threatening loss of contact with important people ("I'll take the kids"); shaming the person for wanting to improve his or her situation (by getting a job, going to school, etc.); withholding money from a spouse or blaming him/her for a weak financial situation; constant complaining before and after a spouse goes out, so that having friends hardly seems worth the hassle; possessiveness (making accusations, badgering or excessive questioning, punishing for eye contact with members of the opposite sex, taking the keys or distributor cap from the car). What's significant about these kinds of abuse is that they usually take the form of a process that begins small and increases over a long period of time.

The message. Abuse, in whatever form, is extremely shaming. Sexual abuse relays the message: "My needs are the most important thing. You are someone to be used, and it doesn't matter if you don't like it." Sexual abuse, where there is a "Can't-talk" rule and a threat ("Keep quiet, or else!"), is doubly shaming to the victim. It relays the message: "I'm doing this bad thing to you because you're worthless. In fact, you're so worthless that I can do whatever I want to you and get away with it."

Victims have a hard time reporting the abuse or even talking about it for a number of reasons. Often they feel responsible. For instance, most battered women feel they somehow deserve the abuse.[3] Often victims say, "I should have known better than to go there, to say this, or do that," as if they are to blame for the abuse. None say, "I am more valuable than that, and I didn't deserve to be treated that way." In addition, they are afraid of what people will think, of what the perpetrator will do, or that no one will believe them. Many of my clients have actually been asked by family, friends, clergy and other counselors, "What do you think you said or did to cause this to happen to you?" Let me ask a question: What's a good enough reason to excuse abuse? There is *no* reason good enough.

Maria was sexually abused early in her adolescence. Legally, what happened to her is called rape. Only after months of therapy was she able to see that she was not the cause of the abuse just because she was infatuated with an older boy, or because she trusted him not to abuse her, or for being at the friend's house where the rape occurred. Could she have made other choices in this situation? Perhaps. But there is no combination of wrong choices that add up to a "good enough" reason for someone to be raped.

All abuse is a violation of the inner boundary of another. An inner boundary is an invisible line inside, which, when crossed, violates a sense of well-being or worth. Abuse occurs when, knowing these boundaries exist, they are nonetheless consciously crossed so that hurt or punishment occurs, or force is used to meet the desires of the offender. In fact, an abusive impact occurs even when boundaries are crossed unintentionally.

If a woman threatens her ex-husband, telling him she will refuse him child-visitation rights unless he does thus and so, that is abusive

---

[3]Kay Marshall Strom, *In the Name of Submission* (Portland: Multnomah Press, 1986), 36.

behavior, and a violation of personal boundaries. If an older sibling ignores the cries of a younger sibling and demands that she play sexual games, or else . . . , that is abuse and a violation of personal boundaries.

In cases of sexual abuse, personal boundaries are violated by the wrong person in an inappropriate way and at an inappropriate time. The result in the victim is a sense of confusion about appropriate sexual boundaries. They question their right to even have boundaries, sexual and otherwise.

Abuse relays the message, "I can do this to you because I'm bigger (or stronger, faster, louder, male, etc.) You're defective and powerless to prevent this from happening. You're responsible for this abuse because of your lack of performance. You're only getting what you deserve. You're also responsible to stop it by performing differently."

The bottom-line message of all forms of abuse is: "Your needs don't matter. Your feelings don't matter. What you think doesn't matter. *You are defective and you are the problem.*"

Suicide

The meaning. I believe suicide takes place when a person gets skilled enough at hating himself. It's the most extreme result of the process set in motion by shame. When someone takes his own life, or even attempts to do so, anyone who cares about him is going to be affected. *Nevertheless,* suicide makes a statement about the choice and behavior of the victim: It says, "This is the way I have decided to deal with my pain."

Survivors will feel sadness, confusion, hurt and a host of other emotions. They'll miss the victim. They may feel angry at themselves and others. At some point, perhaps not immediately, they'll be angry with the victim, as well. They might feel afraid for themselves or others they know. "If I failed to notice how much he was hurting, who *else* might I be failing to notice?" They may also experience some depression. All of these emotions are normal, healthy, human responses to a terrible loss. A healthy grief process will eventually resolve them.

The message. For some survivors, however, a very unhealthy connection is made. A message is internalized. It is as though, through suicide, the victim has said to the survivor, "You're not valuable or important enough for me to stick around. I don't care how you feel. You're somehow responsible for what's happened and you're powerless to change it." The victim's real statement, "I hate myself," translates into "I hate you!"

Clients' statements to me indicate that the shaming message of suicide does get through. "If I were a better dad (mom, friend, pastor, counselor), this wouldn't have happened. I shouldn't have done this or said that. They committed suicide because of me." Sometimes the victim has even left a note that blames other people directly.

Another common reaction of a survivor is this: "I should have known." The truth is that most people who commit suicide *do* signal their intention one way or another. But, often, the meaning of certain actions or conversations becomes clear only *after* the tragedy—the friends or family ignored or misinterpreted the meaning of certain signals unintentionally. Depression, chemical use, withdrawal, the sudden dispersing of personal belongings, or direct threats of suicide were interpreted as having a lesser significance. Even in those cases where the victim gave no signals whatsoever, survivors believe they should have known.

The bottom-line message perceived by survivors is: "Something's wrong with me. I'm a bad person because I was unable to give help." Oftentimes a survivor experiences such shame that he tells himself, "It should have been me." Sometimes this results in their own attempt to eradicate shame with the same "solution," or by turning to other harmful ways of escape.

A Comment

The comment that opened this chapter was made to Anita by her dad many years before her death. It could have been made by her brother, a friend, a boyfriend, a grandparent—it wouldn't have mattered. A great irony in all of this is that Anita was not overweight. An even greater irony, however, is that he was a loving dad, a dad who respected his daughter. He wasn't *trying* to shame her, or to compare her to anyone he admired more. He wasn't trying to get her to lose weight. He was only kidding, and he was oblivious to the fact that his comment had punctured her soul like a dart.

Anita was wounded. A comment intended as a show of affection had been received as an indictment. The fact that it came from a person who was important to her gave the comment its power. Others laughed when he said it: more power. No apology: more power. Anita's adolescent body was going through a major transition and she was already very self-conscious: more power. To complicate things even more, Anita's style of handling problems and pain was to try harder. Therefore, the comment was taken as a challenge.

It seems that the very moment Anita began to define herself as an overweight person, other things took on different meaning in her life as well. Understanding problems and solutions became simple. *She* was the problem: that became a "grid" through which everything in her life was filtered.

The opinions of others shamed her. Her weight shamed her—as did her body, pictures of models in catalogs, even mannequins in store windows. The solution was to stop eating. She even experienced a sense of shame every time she was hungry. She also became depressed because she seemed powerless to bring this "weight problem" under control. This added to her depression: people who are starving experience a physical, mental and emotional "shut-down."

At first, others complimented her on how good she looked. She didn't trust their motives and didn't believe their compliments. Later, they began to express concern. Anita interpreted their concern as an indictment on her solution and, therefore, an indictment on her. She began to withdraw from friends and family. Emotionally and psychologically, she "disappeared" by losing more weight.

At this point, the family intervened and brought her to a therapist. No one could believe the therapist's evaluation that Anita's depression was a result of anorexia, an emotional disorder. Everyone believed the opposite to be true, that the lack of appetite was *caused* by depression. Sessions with another therapist culminated in Anita being given an anti-depressant; it also got her a lot of attention she didn't want. She forced herself to eat and threw herself into school work and activities.

No one understood that Anita's accomplishments only served to refocus people's attention from a set of negative outside behaviors to a set of positive outside behaviors. No one but Anita knew that her shame and pain remained, despite her positive facade. No one could have believed the chain of events begun by an innocent, yet ignorant, comment made in jest so long ago. One day Anita "disappeared" once and for all, and everyone said it was senseless.

But lots of things begin to make sense once you understand the power and the effects of shame.

Perhaps one of the hardest forms of abuse to understand and to recognize is what I call "spiritual abuse." It is to this subject that we will now turn.

6

Spiritual Abuse

Not so long ago, our daughter, Erin, came upstairs with an urgent request. Her younger sister Callie had a pad of paper that Erin wanted. She wanted Mom to tell Callie to hand it over.

"Is it yours?" my wife asked.

"No."

"Have you asked her if you could have it?" Holly continued.

"No."

"Then try asking Callie yourself," Holly suggested. "Maybe she'll decide to share it with you." Erin disappeared downstairs.

I happened to be walking by just then and, as we listened at the top of the stairs, here's what we heard: "Mommy says you're supposed to give me that pad."

Holly called Erin back upstairs: "I heard what you told your sister. I feel very angry when you use *my* name to get your sister to do what *you* want her to do."

Just about every child tries to do this—and so do most adults. When we feel that we don't have enough power on our own to make something happen, we try to "pull strings" with higher authorities.

Since that event at home, I haven't been able to stop thinking about how it applies to "the family of Christians," that is, we who make up the church, the body of Christ. I've wondered if Christ becomes angry when Christians use *His* name to get others to do what *they* want. I'm afraid that a lot of terrible, wounding things are being done to God's people in His name.

It seems that, more often than not, the spiritual issue with which my clients struggle isn't a question of *whether* or not there is a God. It's a matter of fearing that there is—and they're angry because of ways they've been treated by those who use His name. Most of our failure to love and trust God stems from our pictures of God as unlovable and untrustworthy. And most of our anger against Him is not really against the true God but against our unchristian or subchristian concepts of God.[1] God's Word has been used by others on His struggling people to instruct them—not to deal with their problems, but to act "spiritual" regardless of what's real ("fake it till you feel it"). Instead of offering broken people grace and rest, religious systems have handed out standards of religious performance as their solution. Tired, wounded people have been offered religious formulas, not God's unconditional love and acceptance. Consequently, many times they're more tired and depressed than when they first sought the help.

Spiritual Abuse Is Alive—But Not "Well"

Without trying to minimize other forms of abuse, I believe there is a kind of abuse that has the potential of being the most devastating. This abuse occurs in the religious arena and wounds people spiritually. It's one of the most deeply shaming forms of mistreatment and perhaps *the* most difficult to untangle. I will simply call it spiritual abuse.

There are many victims of spiritual abuse. While they feel abused, most people would never call it that. Those who dare to speak out are labeled disobedient, disloyal, contentious, unspiritual, judgmental, critical, or even crazy. Most victims think they are the only ones who have ever had the experience. They're convinced that others wouldn't understand or even believe them. Let me illustrate what I mean by spiritual abuse.

Fred and Jane were removed as adult education coordinators by church leaders simply because they questioned their pastor about something he had said. That made them "disloyal." Eventually, they were run out of the church altogether.

In another instance, a man I'll call John, who was struggling with his sexuality, was taken advantage of sexually by his pastor. When he exposed the abuse, he was harassed by others in the congregation for having the problem in the first place. He was called "judgmental" of the pastor and was driven out. After all, the pastor had come with high praises from the denomination. (But it was later discovered that those denominational leaders were aware of the pastor's previous abuse of young boys and had done nothing about it.)

Jackie, a youth minister, made the "mistake" of telling her senior

---

[1]David Seamands, *Healing of Memories*, 106.

pastor that she felt a little overwhelmed and wanted to cut back for a while. The next thing she knew, she was fired in front of the whole congregation at a church business meeting because she wasn't "spiritual" enough.

"Disobedient" congregations are shamed in God's name week after week, cajoled to attend, to serve, to give money, or build buildings so their leaders can gain a sense of satisfaction.

How Spiritual Abuse Works

There is a phenomenon in family systems that very closely parallels a phenomenon that occurs in spiritual family systems: I'm talking about incest. The similarities between spiritual abuse and incest are astounding. In a healthy, functional family system the parents are there as resource—that is to help and equip the kids. Their purpose is to use their position of power and authority to equip children for adulthood by serving, building and providing need-meeting experiences, messages and relationships for the children.

In many families, however, what the kids think, how they feel, and what they want or need doesn't matter. The children's needs go unmet. In these dysfunctional family systems the children are there to meet the needs of the adults. When this happens sexually, we call it incest.

Incestuous parents use their position of power to gratify their own needs without regard to the harm done to others.[2] Through incest, an adult tries to meet his own needs for importance, power, intimacy, value, or sexual gratification. He is attempting to find fulfillment through the sexuality of the very people whom he is there to protect, build and serve. The place that is supposed to be the *most* safe for a child becomes the *least* safe.

In a healthy, functional church system, God is the Source of acceptance, love and value. The pastor, leaders and teachers are there as the helpers and equippers of the other members. Their job, as in a family, is to use their positions of power and authority to equip members for the work of service by serving, building and providing need-meeting experiences, messages and relationships.

There are some religious systems, however, where what the people think, how they feel and what they want or need doesn't matter.

---

[2]Heitritter and Vought, *Helping Victims of Sexual Abuse* (Bethany House Publishers), 70.

Their needs go unmet. In these dysfunctional systems the members are there to meet the needs of the leadership. When this happens in the spiritual area, it amounts to spiritual abuse.

Where there is spiritual abuse there are people who, through spiritual means, attempt to meet their own needs for importance, power, intimacy, value, or spiritual (really, self-related) gratification. They attempt to find spiritual fulfillment through the religious performance of the very people whom they are there to build up and serve.

When anyone with a position of power and authority uses that power to manipulate, or to shame others into performing, it is spiritually (also emotionally and psychologically) damaging. Again, this is wounding to the victim. And the place that's supposed to be the *most* safe for people becomes the *least* safe.

Abuse in the Old Testament

The abuse of people at the hands of religious leaders is documented throughout the Scriptures.

In Jeremiah 5:26–31, for instance, the prophet relays a series of God's charges against the house of Israel: "For wicked men are found among My people; . . . therefore they have become great and rich . . . they judge not with justice the cause of the fatherless, to make it prosper, and they do not defend the rights of the needy. . . . An appalling and horrible thing has happened in the land." God laments. "The *prophets* prophesy falsely, and the *priests* rule at their direction; my people love to have it so. . . ." (emphasis mine).

Jeremiah 6:13,14 says, "For from the least to the greatest of them, every one is greedy for unjust gain; and from *prophet* to *priest*, every one deals falsely. *They have healed the wound of My people lightly,* saying, 'Peace, peace,' when there is no peace" (emphasis mine). In an abusive religious system, as in any other, the most important thing is to keep the surface smooth and peaceful. The ugly, messy relational process of meeting people's real needs gets sacrificed for a better-looking but *false* sense of peace.

Abuse in the Gospels

Many pictures of spiritual abuse are also painted in the Gospels. Perhaps the most obvious is found in Matthew 23:4: Jesus says of the religious leaders, "They tie up heavy loads, and lay them on men's shoulders; but they themselves are not willing to move them with so much as a finger" (NASB). In Matthew 9:36 we read that Jesus had compassion for the crowds because they were "distressed" and "downcast." The indication is that some external force was distressing and discouraging the people, and as a result they became increasingly tired and downcast.

It is interesting to note by comparison what Jesus said about His own ministry: "Come to Me, all who labor and are heavy-laden, and I will give you rest. Take my yoke upon you, and learn from Me; for I am gentle and lowly in heart, and you will find rest for your souls. For my yoke is easy, and my burden is light" (Matt. 11:28–30). Jesus lets us know that an identifying characteristic of His ministry, and of those who are one with Him, is this: Burdens are lifted from the backs of the tired and heavy-laden and they find rest.

The truth is, "try-hard" and "do-right" religion offers a God that doesn't lift burdens, and He adds more burdens that are potentially worse.

Abuse in the Epistles

The Apostle Paul also saw this abuse happening in his day. Perhaps the most illuminating example of the dynamic of spiritual abuse is the example in the book of Galatians. The Good News had been preached to the people in an area called Galatia. Folks were gloriously saved by grace through faith in Jesus. After Paul left the churches that were established there, certain people followed behind him, spreading a teaching concerning circumcision.

And why were they teaching this doctrine? Was it simply the right thing to do? Galatians 6:13b reads: ". . . they desire to have you circumcised, *that they may glory in your flesh.*" In other words, if others did as they said, it would make them look good; and they would be able to "glory in," or get a sense of value from the religious performance of others. The abusive dynamic is clear. Here we have religious teachers attempting to meet their own needs for respect by coercing the Galatians into legalistic religious performance. This is upside down.

Throughout the book of Galatians, Paul catalogs the damage. He calls what has happened to the Christians at Galatia "persecution" (4:29). They were "troubled" (1:7), the meaning of which ranges from "thrown into mental confusion" to "urged to commit treason." Paul says they had been "bewitched" (3:1), which means it was as if they had a spell put on them. He says they were "hindered" from obeying the truth" (5:7). He calls the teaching an attempt to "bring us into bondage" (2:4). Subject to a "yoke of slavery" (5:1) is his description of living under this teaching. And finally, he asks the sad and telling question—to us and to them: "Where then is that sense of blessing you had?" (4:15, NASB).

Have you ever felt that Christianity promised you freedom, but you feel more enslaved to standards you can never live up to?

Abuse in the Church Today

Melanie's mother contracted a potentially fatal illness and spent many weeks in the intensive care unit of her local hospital. Melanie decided to help out at her parents' home for a couple of weeks. While she was there, she herself became very sick. A two-week visit turned into an eight-week ordeal.

When she returned to her home, she found that her husband had given away, sold, or trashed everything she owned. Clothes, personal belongings—everything! What he did was certainly disrespectful, inconsiderate, degrading and absolutely abusive.

Melanie's wounds were compounded when she shared what had happened with the people from her church. When she spoke of how sad and hurt she felt, she was told, "You wouldn't be so upset if you weren't so occupied with material possessions. You should 'seek first His kingdom, and His righteousness; and all these things will be added to you.' Trust God, instead of feeling sorry for yourself."

When I told her that what had been done to her was wrong, she sobbed and sobbed. She had tried to be "spiritual" and denied her pain—for *eight years!*—all the while too ashamed to talk about or deal with her hurt.

Thomas grew up in a strict religious family and was spiritually abused by his father in several ways. He had a stormy adolescence and acted out his anger by using chemicals and running away—both unhealthy and ineffective ways of dealing with life. In response, his father constantly reminded him that he would have been stoned for acting that way if he had lived in the Old Testament times. His father told him that he was earning a ticket to Hell by having friends who worshiped in other churches, by taking communion in other churches, by liking certain styles of music, and by everything else that he did differently than the way his father wanted.

Later, when Thomas did realize some of the wrongs he had done, he tried to apologize to his parents, but they refused.

Today, Thomas struggles with God's grace and forgiveness and constantly wonders if he is doing good enough religious things. God— and even church buildings—are *very* scary for him.

Kay, at the suggestion of a church elder, had gone to speak to her pastor and his wife about some personal problems. Over the course of the next several months there were numerous times when the pastor's wife couldn't be present at the meetings. During those times of absence, her pastor progressively abused her. He eyed her up and down during the sessions and made sexual remarks, making her feel very uncomfortable. He talked about his own unsatisfactory sex life and was soon touching her and kissing her, first on the cheeks and then on the lips. Eventually, he fondled her and engaged in sexual intercourse with her right in the parsonage.

The pastor's actions were obviously unprofessional, exploitive, abusive, and even illegal.

The incredible progression of Kay's abuse was not over when she quit seeing the pastor. She told her friends in the church, but they wouldn't believe her because the pastor had a solid record after many years in that church. When she confronted the pastor he said, "Who are people going to believe: a basket-case like you, or a highly re- spected pastor like me?"

She opened her heart to another pastor, but he asked her what she'd done to encourage her pastor to act that way. He told her to "turn the other cheek" and forgive him.

Finally, she got up the courage to tell the elder who had sent her to the pastor for counseling, hoping for support from church leader- ship. He responded, "I want you to know you are slandering a friend of mine. He is well-respected, and has had a profound impact on the lives of hundreds of people."

I know he certainly had a profound impact on the life of my client.

There is also another kind of spiritual abuse that can occur even in good Christian homes where the parents truly want to serve the Lord. When I first went into the ministry full-time, my wife and I re- ceived what amounted to a warning letter from a friend. He had grown up in a family whose lives revolved around the ministry of his father. I've chosen a few excerpts from that letter to document some of our friend's pain:

> Dear Jeff and Holly,
>
> It's good to hear about what you're involved in. I've been surrounded by Christian organizations since I was a child, since my father developed quite a few.

Recently, with the help of therapy, I have been dealing with the anger and loss I have felt through the years because of the priority my parents placed on the Christian organizations over members of the family. When I tried to talk to them about it, I was discounted and shamed. My devotion to God was questioned. I am realizing now that it's okay to have needs and feelings—it was never God who was disturbed by how I felt.

My friend had been given the message that serving God was enough of a reason for his dad to neglect the family. Like many others from ministry-oriented families I've seen since then, he had learned to resent and distrust the God who "needed" his parents more than he did.

Preventing Abuse

There are certain things you can do to keep yourself from being abused spiritually.

First, pay attention to your heart. That's where God's Spirit lives. Do you feel respected and safe with your pastor, counselor, or spiritual leader? If you don't, maybe your "radar" is right. Do you have to perform religious behaviors in order to earn love and acceptance, or is it a gift on the basis of Christ's performance? Do the messages you hear (both spoken and unspoken) urge you to try harder to be good—or do they encourage you to depend more upon God as the Source of your life and your needs?

Now I want to caution you. Please—every time your pastor or Bible study leader speaks firmly to you or doesn't accept your view, do not label him or her as spiritually abusive. It's a human trait to react defensively or to be slow in accepting opinions that are not ours. If you have a problem with the way things are being conducted, go to your leader in a gentle, humble spirit and share your thoughts. In a safe system, your confrontation should be welcomed, even if there is not full agreement. However, change takes time, so if you are rebuffed, don't automatically flash accusations. Watch the emphasis in your church or group—is it on how things look, on keeping the peace, and on external religious performance? Beware! Is the system governed by unspoken rules? Is it unsafe and "unspiritual" to talk about problems, feelings or struggles, or even to *have* them? Do you feel more ashamed, tired and wounded as time goes by? Is more effort spent hiding problems in the dark than working them through in the light?

Pay attention to these signs. You may be involved in an abusive, shame-based church or other religious organization similar to those previously described.

Stopping Abuse

Remember that *nice* is never better than *honest*. Remember, too, that the truth is *never* the problem; the problem is *always* the problem. Therefore, if you find yourself being abused spiritually, say so. Confront the abuser. If you don't feel you are strong enough or you are afraid, have someone you trust go with you. If the abusive person won't listen, tell the people to whom the abuser is accountable. This could include the leaders in your local church, leaders from the denomination, or a board that governs or evaluates credentials. *If the abuse is illegal* (sexual or physical), report it to the police. It's okay to hold other people in the church accountable for their illegal behaviors. The laws of the land were instituted by God to protect victims and hold perpetrators accountable (see Romans 13).

If the abuse is not illegal, and therefore not something to be dealt with by the police, the leaders or those responsible must listen to you and deal with the problem. If they don't or won't, and you are treated as if *you* are the problem, *get out of there!* This includes a counseling relationship, a Bible study group, a church, or a religious organization. *Leave,* and look for a group with which you feel safe and can receive some help and healing.

Leadership, power, buildings, programs, organizations, or agendas are not bad in and of themselves. In fact, they are needed to accomplish the work of the church or group. In some religious systems, however, the people have to perform in order to serve the building or organization, or to build up the "spiritual self-esteem" of the leadership.

There are plenty of good churches and Christian leaders who can love, help and equip you. If you need to find a new church home, or a new Christian counselor, don't expect "perfect," but do expect to find one who can help lift the burden from you. God has a spiritual home base that's right for you, and leaders you can trust.

Be willing to make a change, and I believe you'll find a place to root and grow that's best for you.

Now that we've examined messages that bring shame, the process and causes, we will redirect our focus slightly to look at the effects shame has on individuals.

For many who feel defective, a strange phenomenon occurs. One day they may feel up, ready to take on the world and win! The next day they can feel down, ready to give up. This is not borderline manic-depression, it is simply a cycle that develops in people who feel shame.

For many who are stuck in this "give-up/try-hard" cycle, the chapter that follows may provide the first accurate picture of what's going on inside, and help those to understand why they do the unexplainable things they do.

---

*Spiritual abuse is dealt with more completely in the book *The Subtle Power of Spiritual Abuse* by David Johnson and Jeff VanVonderen, published by Bethany House Publishers.

7

I Feel As Though It's Never Enough

George dragged himself into my office and slumped down in a chair. He was silent for quite some time. With a downcast look, he finally said, "I didn't want to come in today. I just want to give up. Don't you get tired of me?"

"What's going on, George?" I asked.

"I was doing so well again—like last September," came the reply. "But this week I got back into behaviors I thought I'd left behind for good. I feel so ashamed. I wish I knew what was going on."

I knew what was going on. George was on the low end of a cycle I've come to recognize in most of my counseling clients—the "give-up/try-hard" cycle. I had seen George on this "down-stroke" before. Just seven weeks earlier he had been overcome with shame and despair. Then came victory and vindication. Through sheer, white-knuckle will-power, George had managed to grind out six weeks of abstinence from some very unhealthy sexual behaviors that had preoccupied his life for years. That sent his self-esteem sky-rocketing; George was convinced he was on top of his problem forever. The week before this particular session, however, he'd run out of self-effort fuel and crashed once more. Now, weary and ashamed, he wanted to give up.

Introducing the Cast

In theater, "irony" is characters working toward one goal, but obtaining the opposite result. To grasp the irony in the life drama of the shame-based person, it's necessary to meet the cast that plays in the inner drama of each one who suffers from the effects of shame. (You'll understand the irony a little later.)

Giving Up

There are five integral characters who provide the energy for *both* the "give-up" side and the "try-hard" side of this cycle. First is the *outside source,* delivering shaming messages about the person. Second are the *messages* that shame. The third character in the cycle is the *mind* of the person who looks at himself as defective and shamed. Fourth is the person's resulting *behavior.* And finally, there are the *cheerleaders*, that is, other people involved in the person's life who shout messages to him from the sidelines. Let's define these more specifically, one by one, as we see how the cycle works.

The Outside Source

Outside
Source

Some people have come from parent/ child relationships that were overtly shaming. By that, I mean there was name-calling, comparing, put-downs, favoritism, perfectionism, sideways communication, shaming rules and rejection.

One thirty-year-old client, whom I'll call Dal, told me about growing up in a relationship with a stepfather and stepbrother. Very often, the two of them would do things together and not include Dal. With great difficulty, he told me how it was when they *did* include him. The three of them would be watching television, for instance, and Dal's stepfather would ask his own son if he wanted something to drink. Or he'd leave the room and return with popcorn for just the two of them.

Rejection had left a shame wound in this man. "What's wrong with *me?*" Dal asked me through tears.

Others have come from family systems that were upside-down, where the children were expected to meet the needs of the parents. Many more have been shamed by an abusive spouse or abusive children. Still others bear the shame of living with someone who is addicted to drugs, alcohol, sex, work, or religion.

Many have received messages that shame them from sources outside of their family. Being mugged, beaten or raped is extremely shaming. Nearly sixty percent of all rapes are committed by someone the victim knows, yet only eight percent are reported. How can this be? I suggest that the reason these attacks are not reported is shame. (And in a society that idolizes a *macho* image for men, it's shaming to be a *male victim.*)

Simply making a mistake or being corrected in public can cause feelings of shame. Being passed over for a promotion or raise sends indicting messages to people, as does getting fired, being laid-off or having extended periods of unemployment. Children are shamed when they're teased by peers for getting *F*'s and even *A*'s, or for looking, talking, walking or dressing a certain way.

For many people, attending church is an extremely shaming experience. Performance-based religion shames people for struggling, asking, doubting, feeling, or resting—and for not complying, reading, giving, attending, or doing. For some, the experience of church or the thought of God has such bitter, shaming connotations that they avoid them altogether.

The Messages that Shame

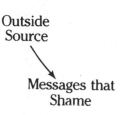

Perhaps this is the easiest part of the cycle to understand. As a result of relationships and experiences with our outside sources, we receive most of our information about who we are as people. When the messages are wounding, we tend to read them like this: Something's wrong with me; I'm a bad person; I can't do anything right; I'm defective, inadequate, selfish, incompetent, worthless, crazy, stupid, in the way; I'm an embarrassment, a mistake, a pest.

The Mind

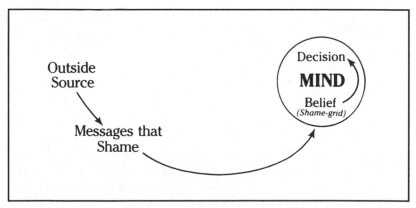

The next character to come on stage is your mind.

Belief. The mind begins with the belief system, or what I earlier referred to as the "shame-grid." This means that you have a belief system or mindset that perpetuates shame. If you are of this mindset, you'll recognize the elements that contribute to the enslaving cycle.

First, you accept the outside source as a reliable, legitimate place from which to find out about yourself. In other words, in order for me to have the power to shame you, you have to believe that I have the power to determine something about your value as a person.

Second, you accept that what I'm saying about you—through words, actions, or our relationship—is actually the truth.

Third, you come to the conclusion that someone who is as bad as you are deserves to feel bad and deserves to be punished. This means that you become the judge and jury and find yourself condemned in the courtroom of your mind.

After years of practice, this pattern has become natural for you. You never question its validity—you accept the message as true.

This leads you to a crossroads—to a point where your will is involved. You must now make some choices about what to do next.

Decision. You now choose: either to give up, or to try harder.

If you conclude that your performance has failed, the situation is hopeless, and you are a shameful, defective individual, you will *give up.* You choose to act in a way that fits best with your assessment of yourself, so you embark on the give-up part of the cycle.

The Behavior

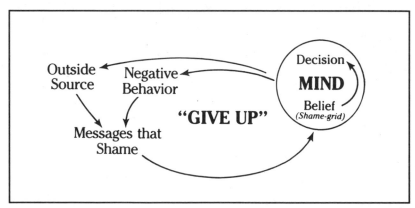

When you act in a way that's consistent with your shame, the cycle is complete. You may—and here's the irony—do exactly the thing you hate doing. This fulfills the outside source's assessment of you, and it was fulfilled because you accepted and acted upon that assessment.

The worst of it is that the cycle isn't complete *yet*. It starts over! You'll tend to stay in relationships that enable you to feel as bad as you "need" to feel. Or you might even perpetuate the bad feelings yourself. The messages of shame are so deeply ingrained into your identity that *you* become the perpetrator.

For instance, Monica had a problem with overeating. When she ate too much (and even when she ate normally), she felt guilty. She also felt like a weak, bad person. She would shame herself by calling herself derogatory names. She'd say, "I should feel bad for being such a weak person and such a pig." Then she would overeat again. Without knowing it, she was simply doing the behavior that allowed her to feel as shamed as she "should" feel for being so "bad."

The Cheerleaders

While this part of the cycle is happening, people in your life observe your behavior and shame you for it:

"What's wrong with you?"

"How can you act that way?"

"You should be ashamed."

"Don't you care what people are thinking about you?"

"Frankly, I'm disappointed in you."

"I thought you would have known better than that."

The cheerleaders compare you to others, quote Bible verses at you, or find a variety of ways to hide or excuse you when someone is looking. They are represented by the figures below. The arrows are their additional shaming messages. The complete cycle looks like this:

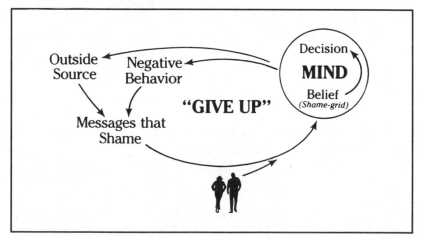

78

Some Practical Examples

Let me further illustrate how the cycle works for someone caught in the trap of shame. By describing the cycle, I don't mean to imply that a person actually thinks these thoughts consciously. Some people may; most, however, experience this as an automatic process.

OUTSIDE SOURCE: A husband batters his wife.

SHAMING MESSAGE: The abuse and blaming says to the victim, "You're so defective I can do this to you. Your needs, feelings and personal boundaries don't matter."

BELIEF: "I'm a defective, bad person. Someone as bad as me deserves to be hurt. I am *not* loved, accepted or capable. Nothing I do is good enough."

DECISION: "What's the use? I don't deserve a healthy relationship, anyway. If I leave, I might end up in a worse situation. I give up."

BEHAVIOR: The victimized wife stays in the relationship and continues to be abused.

OUTSIDE SOURCE: The battering continues.

SHAMING MESSAGE: The abuse and blaming by the perpetrator, plus the victim's own behavior (giving in and accepting the abuse), says to the victim, "It's your fault. What's wrong with you? If you were a sane person, you'd leave."

BELIEF: "I'm a bad person who deserves what I get. No one else would want a relationship with someone like me."

DECISION: "I deserve to get hurt. This serves me right. I'm lucky even to have a relationship."

BEHAVIOR: The victim stays in the relationship and continues to be abused. Chemical use, overeating, undereating, self-abuse, abuse of others, and even suicide may occur at this point as a means of self-punishment for the victim.

You may know someone who has gone from one abusive relationship to another. In frustration you might say, "Why do you keep doing that?" And with equal frustration they'll probably answer, "I don't know!" I am convinced that this cycle explains the behavior.

As you can see from the above illustration, the cycle also escalates. When this person acts out his shame and anger in an abusive way toward himself or his children, his own behavior has begun to generate messages that shame. He behaves in a way that he said he never would. It goes against his values. The outside perpetrator can move away or even die, and the victim will continue to receive shaming messages—his own thoughts and behavior will produce these.

Trying Hard

Trying harder is *not* the way to break the cycle I've just described.

Shame is a master of disguise. What convinced me of this is something I have noticed in counseling. I have seen corporate executives whose marriages are in as much trouble as those of alcoholics. They just *look* better. I have seen pastors who are as shallow and callous as bartenders. They just *look* better. I have seen submissive wives who are just as tired and disillusioned as prostitutes. They just *look* better.

How can this be? Because positive self-effort fails as an adequate source of inner peace and value in the same way that negative self-effort fails as an escape from shame.

In order to understand the "try-hard" side of the cycle, let's take a look at our cast of characters again. The descriptions of the first two cast members—the *outside source* and the *message*—are the same as before. But when the *mind* or shame-grid comes into play, the descriptions appear to be different. Let's check the differences and see how they work.

The Mind

Belief. Here is the point at which you *appear* to respond differently to the shaming message.

You seem to reject the message. At first you react against the validity of the outside source, rejecting it as a legitimate source of messages about you. Second, you react against what the outside source *says* about you. No longer the prosecutor, you become the defense attorney, determined to prove your innocence.

Again, there only *appears* to be a difference. The fact that you have reacted so strongly to the shaming messages, by rejecting them and defending yourself against them, really means that the shame has reached you. Your shame-grid has allowed the shame in, and it is wreaking its havoc. Your response may be different, but the wound is there.

Decision. Now, of course, you must make a choice about what to do next. You can give up, or try harder. At this point, there is a genuine departure from the cycle as we've understood it so far. You're really tired of feeling bad, so you come to a different conclusion. You decide that your performance *can* prove that you are better, the situation *is* hopeful, and you *are* going to establish once and for all that you are a capable, powerful person. You decide to try harder.

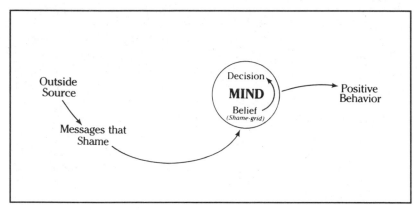

The Behavior

Once you act in a way that's positive and powerful, the "try-hard" side of the cycle has begun.

There are many reasons why you might decide to try harder. Perhaps you're tired of the consequences that result from the "give-up" side of the cycle. You might have a positive turn of events that fills you with hope. You might begin a relationship with a person or group of people who pep-talk you into believing that you really are capable. You may have just attended this year's version of the "try-hard" conference. You might know someone who has struggled with problems similar to yours and has overcome them. Or maybe you're rested up from having given up for so long.

So, your behavior now swings to the opposite of what you did before. If you used to overeat, you undereat. If you used to neglect your Bible reading, you're sure to read it daily—and even get up half-an-hour earlier than usual to do it. If you struggle with pornography, you painstakingly avoid magazine racks and certain movies. If you have a problem with chemical use, you grit your teeth and abstain.

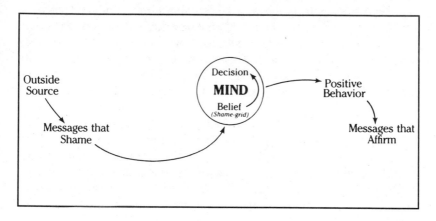

Messages That Affirm

The positive behavior promises a cure to the shame. "You are great, see how capable you are, you are loved and accepted now." Now the cycle should be complete, but it isn't. It simply starts over as these affirming messages deflect off the shame-grid. Finally, of course, the cheerleaders are there to put in their two cents on your life. The final cycle results:

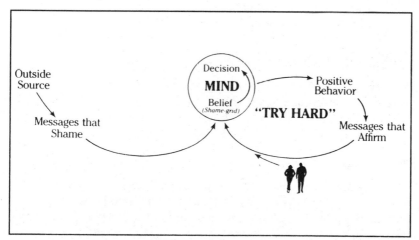

The Irony

Here's where we can see the irony of trying to perform your way out of shame.

Even when affirmations and support come through your shame-grid, your mind rejects the praise. You simply don't believe the messages. What comes through is, "It's not true; I'm still not good enough. I could do better. Besides, if people knew what I'm really like, they wouldn't be giving me all these strokes." Or you push away the validation because "humility" earned a lot of points in the past. Or you were taught that the way to get God to love you was to hate yourself enough.

Do you see that in the depths of your soul your *belief*—your self-appraisal—has not changed? Now comes the time to evaluate and *decide*. Has the effort worked? Do you know you're a valuable, acceptable person? Is everyone pleased? Have you lived up to the standard? Have you proven your family wrong yet? No? "Better try harder," says the inner taskmaster. So you return to more positive *behavior* and the cycle continues.

You've returned to the "try-hard" side of the cycle. But, let's say that instead of this being only the second time it's the *tenth* time. The inner voice is demanding answers: Hasn't this worked yet? Can you finally say you're a valuable, acceptable person? Isn't everyone satisfied yet? Haven't you lived up to the standard yet? Haven't you proven to your family that you can make it yet? Hasn't God seen enough?

You're tired, disillusioned, ashamed. You've run out of self-effort fuel, so you *decide* to give up.

It's back to the "give-up" side of the cycle.

Three Tiring Scenarios

I want to put the cycles described in this chapter into everyday context by describing three types of people that result from buying into the lie that self-effort is the way to healthy self-esteem: the Underachiever, Overachiever, and the Roller-coaster.

The Underachiever

This person spends most or all of his life on the "give up" side of the cycle. He is tired, burned out, disillusioned, depressed, addicted. His addictions look bad and he knows it. He disappears, or wishes he could.

These folks are perpetual underachievers. People around them feel frustrated by the huge disparity between their capabilities and their performance. They either pep-talk them concerning their value, or shame them for not performing. But they simply can't perform their way out of the cycle. No one can have a close relationship with them.

They push people away physically and emotionally, and push God away spiritually. It's because they're doing too poorly right now. They are the ones in families, churches, and society that people take care of—for a while, until they're given up on because of their lack of response. For all the performance-based people around them, they are simply bad for public relations.

Once in a while they find themselves in an environment that shames them for being so defective. Then they swing over to the "try-hard" side, but it doesn't last for long. They are simply out of gas to start with. They merely survive.

The Overachiever

These people never get tired—or at least never let anyone know they are. They live their whole lives on the "try-hard" side of the cycle. They are the go-getters, the shakers and movers, the ones who make things happen. They are energetic, enthusiastic and charismatic. They think that workaholism is better than alcoholism. They think that un-dereating is the solution to overeating. Their addictions look good. They perpetually over-achieve.

People around overachievers feel frustrated because they can't keep up with them. Those who care about them try to get them to rest, but to no avail. Rest is a waste of time. No one can get close to them. They're not in one place long enough. They put people off physically and emotionally and put God off spiritually, because they're too busy doing "important" things right now. They're the ones in families, churches and society that take care of others—for a while at least, until someone doesn't notice, or they don't get the results they want.

Once in a while they simply run out of gas and swing over to the "give-up" side. You've seen it happen. The successful business person who sells everything, gives it away and disappears. Or the acclaimed psychologist who helps hundreds of people for thirty years and then hangs himself. Or that respected clergyman who has preached holy living in the two decades since becoming your pastor, and then splits for the coast one day with the church secretary. When they get caught, they repent, promise it will never happen again, and return to the "try-hard" side.

The Roller-Coaster

The third type of person is the one whose lifestyle vacillates from one side of the cycle to the other, like a roller coaster. Obviously, this is no way to live either. It's a tiring, frustrating and shaming life, characterized by extremes. Love, then hate; hopefulness, then despair; signals that say come close, then stay away. You're just never sure what's next.

This person knows a lot about everything and not much about anything. When they're on the verge of failure they try harder. When they are on the verge of success they give up. They seldom follow through with things about which they give their word, but they come through when nothing is expected or even wanted. People are afraid to get close to them, because they can't be trusted. You never know with whom you are dealing at any given time.

The successes and failures of the roller coaster are mostly determined by their level of self-effort fuel at any given moment. When the energy level is high they try hard, look good, do it all. When they run out of energy they give up and lapse into a state of disillusionment. Once they are rested up, they attend another seminar, read another book, see another therapist, buy another set of tapes and they're on their way again!

Needless to say, there is no victory or progress in the "give-up/try-hard" cycle. The person found on the "give-up" side is a living testimony of the power of shame. The person found on the "try-hard" side is a living testimony to self-righteousness. And the last person, one who flips from one side to the other, is a living testimony to the tiredness that comes from having no god one minute, and yourself as god the next.

Thank God—and I mean that literally—that our Lord *has* a way to set us free. For those who have been badgered by false gods who have caused you to labor under a gospel of shame—it's time for the Good News.

I want to introduce you, maybe for the first time, to the One True God, and to His message of *grace*, which will set you free from the wearying "give-up/try-hard" cycle.

Part II

—

Healed by Grace

Introduction

Chains Do Drop Off

Now it is time to look at each of the elements of the old cycle in the light of God's grace. For it is God's grace, not our striving, that makes us accepted and acceptable. It is His performance in Christ, not our trying hard to perform, that eradicates our shame. By learning to look through a "grace-grid," we'll learn how to fight a different kind of battle than the one we've been trying to win through our own self-effort.

This is going to be a difficult struggle for many. Those of us with shame have a hard time accepting gifts. We try for a long time to "earn" them. What's so wonderful, though, is that we can be loved, accepted, capable, and worthwhile for *free*—because, in love, God purchased our eternal state of "acceptedness" with the blood of His own Son, Jesus Christ.

That's the *real* Good News of the gospel! We'll examine it more closely throughout this section. And along the way, of course, I'll be weaving God's message of grace together with practical steps that will help you become free from the messages of shame and defectiveness that have held you down long enough!

8

Breaking the "Give-Up/Try-Hard" Cycle

The bad news, as we've seen, is that it is impossible to recover from a problem that your relationship system—whether family or church—does not allow you to *admit* or *talk about*. Now, however, you know what the problem is; you know where the problem came from; you know what doesn't work to solve it. The "Can't-talk" rule is being broken, at least within you. You have permission to bring things from darkness into the light. And you're finding out that having experienced what you have, you are completely normal. Let's continue the process with a direct assault on your mental shame-grid.

The battle to recover from shame and live a life of freedom and fullness is waged in two primary arenas: the renewal of the mind, and the fight of faith. This chapter will concentrate on that first arena, the mind.

"Earning" Acceptance and Value Isn't Possible

Scores of clients of all ages have told me of the sense of shame and defectiveness they have felt for *not* doing the things they know they are expected to be doing. If they aren't Christians, they're tired because they know their task is impossible. If they are Christians, they're tired from trying to do what is God's task and not theirs.

Rick is a great example of a Christian who is working hard to "earn" a heavenly wage that's already been credited to his account. Rick looks good—he *always* looks good. He's a shaker and mover in his job and at church. Even at that, I wasn't surprised when he showed up in my office one day and proclaimed, "This abundant life stuff is a crock. I was better off before I was a Christian. At least then I didn't know how bad I was doing."

Time and space would fail me if I tried to list all the people who have said that in one form or another. Ironically, the great majority of people want a secret formula on how to change their behaviors, thereby alleviating their shame. If only they could find some means to live up to God's expectations—which are even higher than all the other expectations that they aren't living up to.

After years of being in the shoes of "the striver," I know some of what Rick is feeling. It's scary and frustrating to know how far short you fall, and yet to think that *you* are your solution. I now understand something about the nature and purpose of God's law—His standard—that I misunderstood for most of my life. One day the light came on. Our church was in the middle of a study of Galatians when I realized that God didn't give the Law so that we could "do good enough," and then pat ourselves on the back for being such good people. He gave the Law to convince us that we *can't* earn God's approval by human effort and to drive us to His gift. As Paul wrote:

> . . . a man is not justified by works of the law but through faith in Jesus Christ . . . because by works of the law shall no one be justified. (Gal. 2:16)

Using the Law Correctly

We've already said that God *didn't* give the Law so we could become right with Him through our own good behavior. Now I'd like to tell you the reasons why God *did* give the Law. I believe it's important for you to grasp this concept fully, otherwise you may just "agree" with my statements, but go away with the sneaking suspicion that God is still waiting for you to goof up so He can scold and punish you.

Actually, Scripture indicates three reasons why the Law was given. They have to do with God's goal, which is to bring people into a relationship with himself. If the Law does what it was given to do, then the establishment of a gift-based relationship between you and God will result. And that's exactly what Paul says:

> For I through the law died to the law, that I might live to God. (Gal. 2:19) Likewise, my brethren, you have died to the law through the body of Christ, so that you may belong to another, to him. . . . (Rom. 7:4)

The greatest misunderstanding concerning the Law comes in the area of our perception of its purpose. Somehow we continue to believe that the Law is God's provision for people to live victoriously. But notice that in Romans 7:4, Paul says the weight of the Law is lifted by Christ, not by our own lawfulness. As a result of that misconception— coupled with personal shame and the drive to obey the law out of a sense of duty or fear—most people come to feel as tired and inadequate as they *should* be feeling!

Why the Law?

First, it is the purpose of the Law to convict people of their shortcomings. The Law was given as a mirror to reflect back to a person the picture that his life is full of sin (falling short or missing the mark). Romans 3:20b says: " . . . through the law [standard] comes knowledge of sin [not living up to the standard]." So, It's *good* when someone realizes, by means of God's mirror, that he is a sinner who has fallen short.

The second purpose of the Law is to convince us that we are helpless to erase our own defectiveness. No one can come to God by following the Law; the Law is too tough and we are inadequate. Paul says, "But the scripture consigned all things to sin" (Gal. 3:22). And Romans 11:32 says, ". . . God has consigned all men to disobedience. . . ." The Greek word for "consigned" in both texts conveys the sense of being locked in prison. The Law was given, then, not so that people could have peace with God by living up to it, but to show that we can't live up to it—we can't be good enough on our own.

The third purpose of the Law is the final one dealing with God's gracious effort to bring people into a relationship with himself. Look at the end of Romans 11:32: "God has consigned all men to disobedience, *that he may have mercy upon all.*" God *has* provided a way of coming into a right relationship with Him. (All mankind's systems are about earning acceptance, proving value, gaining approval. We, however, receive mercy and acceptance through faith, not by earning mercy and acceptance through self-effort.) God is the only one with a system that offers acceptance and value at His own expense.

Jesus declares that faith in Him is the goal of the Law: "Think not that I have come to abolish the law and the prophets; I have come not to abolish them but to fulfill them" (Matt. 5:17).

How does that work? When a person comes to faith in Christ, and makes Him their basis of life, value and identity, it means the Law has done its job. Paul reiterates that this is the reason the Law was given, in Romans 10:4: "For Christ is the end [literally, *goal*] of the law, that every one who has faith may be justified." Conversely, if you are still striving to feel that you are good enough, you are either in a blind bondage to the world's or religion's idols, not realizing you can be free, or you are afraid to put your full trust in Christ—afraid to believe He came to make you acceptable to God, afraid to believe that He has.

Confronting Abusers of the Law

Recently, I heard a sermon on my car radio that illustrates the abuse of the Law very clearly. A well-known radio teacher was preaching on the Ten Commandments. He suggested to the listening audience that we picture a balance scale. We were instructed to place the Ten Commandments on one side of the scale. On the other, we were told to place our obedience to God. He then asked us to see if the scale was heavy on the Commandment side (which it will *always* be). If it was (as he knew it would be), he said we ought to feel ashamed and get busy trying harder to live the way we should. This is *abuse* of God's Law.

In Philippians, Paul warns us to beware of people who sound holy but are really "enemies of the cross" (3:18). When we hear that phrase today we think of atheists, agnostics, or secular humanists who say that the cross isn't real. But the enemies of the cross at Philippi were those who said the cross was *not enough*! My conviction is that similar enemies of the cross are alive and well in churches today.

For a person to assess his life as victorious based upon how well he has followed the Law indicates that his source of satisfaction is derived from his own self-effort. This is idolatrous; it leads to self-righteousness, and it is not what God intended.

The purpose of the Law—let me emphasize—is *not* to control evil people. Read the newspapers to see how incapable law is to restrain lawbreakers. God's Law was given to drive us to grace and hold us there. The victorious life cannot be found *in, under, or through* the Law. It is to be discovered and lived in a "gift-based" environment and through a "gift-based" relationship with Jesus Christ and with others, under *grace*.

Grace

Too often, we hear Christians say things like, "You fell into sin? Well, it's okay. We're under grace." But grace is not God's way of saying that sin doesn't matter. Grace is God saying, "I've already paid the price you're trying to pay. I've already bridged the gap you're trying to bridge. The indictment is gone. We're friends now. In fact, you're my very own. Come on over to me, problems and all, and we'll discover the way through the pain together."

As Paul asked the Galatians, "Let me ask you only this: Did you receive the Spirit by works of the law, or by hearing with faith? Are you so foolish? Having begun with the Spirit, are you now ending with the flesh?" (Gal. 3:2, 3).

The only correct motive for living by God's standards is because you love Jesus and *want* to obey Him. In fact, obedience is the natural result of dependence upon God. Trusting in God to meet your financial needs, for example, may *result* in more generous support of truly worthy causes. Believing that the cross validates you may mean you don't need such a big car or such an expensive house. Knowing you have God's approval may *result* in depending on your own performance (positive *or* negative) less, or in seeking the approval of others. And certainly, there are practical reasons for living by God's Law. Even the lives of non-Christians would improve if they followed the standards of God.

Earning Isn't Necessary

Most people with shame have incredibly negative thoughts playing and replaying in their heads about God, because they have been abused in His Name, and they have been abused by His Law. Ironically, a correct understanding of the Law really can be liberating to those living their lives stuck in the "give-up/try-hard" cycle. To those in the "give-up" mode, the Law declares that the problem with the old, negative self-effort is not the "negative" part but the "self-effort" part.

The solution is resting in what God has already done through Jesus Christ. Ephesians 1:4 says: ". . . He chose us in him before the foundation of the world, that we should be holy and blameless before him."

I can picture God, before the world was created. He looked forward into time and saw your birth and mine. He watched as we grew, through the good times and bad. He saw our stumblings. He saw our wounds. He saw all of our sins. And He saw the myriad ways you and I would try to meet our own needs and overcome our pain—each of them falling short.

His choosing us *then* causes you and me to be holy and blameless before Him *now*. Before you and I were even born, He decided to do whatever it took to rescue us and to make it possible for us to hit the mark. Since we couldn't afford that heavy payment, He paid for it with His Son. And since we couldn't earn it, He gave it as a gift.

For those of us who have lived out the "try-hard" solution to shame, there *is* another option. We can learn to rest in who we are and what is ours because of what God has done. It is out of that rest that we perform, at His loving direction. But in order to do that, we have to change our minds about some things.

At this point a decision has to be made. Now that you understand the problem more clearly and can see what the solution *isn't,* you need to decide right now to reject *your performance* as having any power to indict or vindicate you. Because it's only at the place where we have *no* performance that God's performance begins to make sense. It's only at the place where earning acceptance through self-effort looks as bankrupt as it is that "gift-based" acceptance, value and identity can look as good and powerful and liberating as it truly is.

Introducing the "Rest" Cycle

After taking a look again at the diagrams for the "give-up/try-hard" cycle (ch. 7), note that the new "rest cycle" begins in the middle of the old cycle, where there is no performance on your part. It begins after your last behavior and before your next. It begins in the mind, that place where you believe and decide things. Throughout the remainder of this book, I am simply going to present information for you to think about and consider. If you disagree with it or don't believe it, you can always go back to your old solutions. But, I hope you don't do that. I hope that you can keep an open mind, and find the place where you can truly *rest*. God has a gift for you.

Meet the Characters

God's gift absolutely and irrevocably contradicts and obliterates everything in the message that says that you and I are defective and unworthy of any attention or love. Instead of the old, shaming sources, He becomes our new Source of messages about ourselves. God's stance toward wounded, tired people is one of compassion, grace and forgiveness. As our Father, He is our healer and provider. Although we may have had parents who rejected us, we have a Father who has chosen us, just as we are. As the Holy Spirit, He is our Comforter and Helper. We are never alone because of His continuing and indwelling presence. He is the proof of God's settled acceptance of you and me. As the flesh-and-blood Son, God demonstrated His love and compassion through both His life and death. Through the cross, the penalty of all our guilt was paid once and for all, and we have been rescued from death and destruction and shame.

Now there are *new messages* about ourselves to consider. We are loved, accepted, lovable and acceptable—and not because of any laws we've kept or spiritual merit badges we've earned. We are brand new creations—clean, innocent, blameless—no longer under indictment. We are His heirs.

Consequently, our fight is no longer a fight to produce better behavior, but it is characterized by fighting to *believe* what is true about us because of what God has done; it's a fight to *decide* to live in a manner that's consistent with these new messages. Now, our behavior is a result of the process of transformation that comes from the renewing of our mind and accepting our acceptance. The following diagram illustrates it:

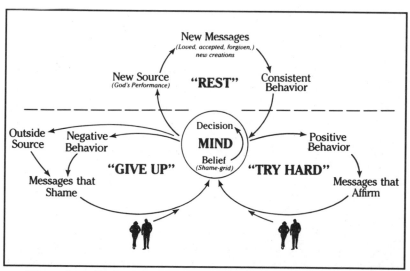

Now we will flesh out the steps of this "rest cycle" in greater detail.

9

God Says You Don't Have to Live in Shame

Recently, a man we'll call Don came in for a counseling session and explained that his fifth extramarital affair hadn't worked out the way he'd planned. He was depressed, his blood pressure was high, he'd developed a peptic ulcer and he wasn't sleeping. He was also so ashamed that he couldn't look me in the eye. "What should I do?" he begged.

"First of all, let go of the relationship," I suggested. "Then start asking *why* you keep having affairs. Is it that you think adultery is okay?"

"No," he replied, "but I can't let her go. She's all I have going for me. Otherwise, I'm nothing."

"Then maybe you need to have a few more affairs. Maybe the problem is that you just haven't had *enough* affairs."

He was shocked.

What do *you* think? Do you think Don has tried hard enough?

A woman we'll call Betty came in for counseling just a week ago and told me that she's been teaching Sunday school for twenty years. It's been sheer drudgery for the last ten. She has no joy in teaching the class—no excitement about the content, no patience or energy with the kids. She can't look me in the eye either. "What should I do?" she pleaded.

"First of all, quit teaching," I offered. "Then start asking *why* you keep doing something you dislike so much."

"I can't quit," she said. "It's the only thing I'm doing for the Lord. And what would happen to the kids? Who will do it if I don't?"

"Then maybe you just need to teach for a few more years. Maybe you just haven't taught enough classes yet."

I thought she was going to collapse beneath the weight of that suggestion.

What do *you* think? Do you think Betty has tried hard enough?

Both of these very tired people are using up a lot of energy trying to escape from their sense of defectiveness. They are attempting to fill their inner emptiness from outer sources. As those sources fail to provide what they *really* need, they try harder. Is lack of effort the culprit behind their tiredness? No. The culprit is shame.

There are four aspects involved in the shame phenomenon that you must understand in order to grasp its depth and the reasons why it's so difficult to escape: the problem, the solution, the enemy, and the battle.

1. Problem

At the crux of the shame issue is a sense of personal defectiveness. Webster's dictionary gives the definition of defective as "incomplete or deficient." A person with shame views himself as defective, as someone who lacks love or acceptance (*deficient* even in those qualities that might make him lovable or acceptable). He also sees himself as lacking in importance, credibility, and in the support of those around him—in short, deficient in worth and ability. For a person like this, life is an endless struggle to earn love and acceptance, to prove his worth, to acquire value, to gain importance, and to find meaning to his existence.

The following diagram illustrates how the shame-based *identity* is the dilemma.

As you can see, a shame-based identity is like soil that's capable of producing a variety of plants. The point here is that the "soil" itself is the primary problem, not the plants. We are talking about the issue of man's fundamental identity. The problem every one of us grapples with is an inner problem—not what we *have* on the inside, but what we *lack*. Initially, we lack *life*, and the ability to gain it through any efforts of our own.

Life and Death

In Genesis 2, we read that God created Adam and Eve and placed them in a garden filled with every resource to meet their needs. Everything in the garden was for their benefit and enjoyment—except the tree of the knowledge of good and evil. As we know all too well, Adam and Eve ate from that tree. And they died.

But death and life are not exactly opposites. Dying is the loss of something, the loss of life. In *Birthright*, David Needham describes mankind's life and death dilemma after the Garden of Eden incident, ". . . the Bible focuses in on what they (Adam and Eve) *lost* rather than on what they acquired."[1] When you die, it isn't that you've gotten something. Being dead is *lacking* something; it's lacking life. The fifth chapter of Romans uses several words to paint a picture of mankind's dilemma outside of a relationship with God through Christ, illustrated by the following diagram:

The person represented in the diagram is dead (lacking life), helpless (lacking the ability to change his situation), and a sinner (falling short of God's standard). All of which underscores mankind's defectiveness. Even printing the words inside the circle is misleading, because the circle should be totally empty. Remember, this person's problem is not what he has; it's what he lacks.

I don't believe that people consciously choose to remain dead. But that is exactly what Don and Betty, whom I mentioned at the beginning of this chapter, are doing. Of course, it's easier to see how Don is choosing death, because what he's doing is an obvious sin. (Galatians 6:7 says: "Do not be deceived; God is not mocked, for whatever a man sows, that he will also reap.") But Betty is actually in the same boat, because she is choosing to seek life from a service that can't give her life—even if it looks good. So, unwittingly, she is choosing to remain dead. Both of them are reaping what self-effort always yields: shame, tiredness, and death.

---

[1]David Needham, *Birthright* (Multnomah, 1979), 20.

Trying to Find Life

The fact that we as humans lack life, that we even sense the absence of it, can be witnessed by looking at others around us. Just read the newspaper for a chronicle of the ways people try to get life from sources that can't give it. For that matter, read the Bible. The Scriptures document case after case of how people tried to find life, value and meaning from sex, power, conquest of kingdoms, money, false gods and religion. And these accounts are not talking about the "heathen."

Abraham thought a son would give him meaning, so he acquired one in his own way, instead of waiting for God to keep His promise. King Saul sought life through power. David looked to a woman. In the garden of Gethsemane, Peter turned macho and drew a sword on a squadron of temple guards; then got weak-kneed and denied Jesus in order to hold on to the acceptance of the crowd. Ananias and Sapphira trusted in money. For the Galatians it was circumcision. For the Corinthians it was boasting about their pastor and the gifts the Spirit had given them. Saul, before he became the apostle Paul, relied on his religious heritage and performance. Revelation 2 tells us that the Ephesians left their first love and became a bunch of good-deed-doers.

In the next illustration, I want to build on the previous one by enclosing the smaller circle of emptiness within a larger circle. This outer circle represents external sources from which men and women try to find inner life and fullness:

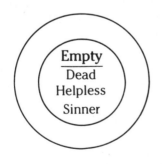

Now let's develop the illustration a bit further by filling in the outside circle with the behaviors by which people attempt to be valuable and acceptable. These behaviors can be positive or negative or neutral. The (+) represents those behaviors that are positive— helping others, giving money, going to church, feeding the poor, and reading your Bible all qualify for this category. Included in this category would be the bad behaviors a person *does not* indulge in: "I don't drink, smoke, gamble, commit adultery, etc." Betty's circle would be full of (+) signs.

The (−) stands for those behaviors we would typically call

sins. These include rape, murder, cheating, lying, stealing, taking God's name in vain, and sexual sins, among others. These also include the good behaviors a person *does not* do. Don's circle would be full of (−) signs. The (?) represents a behavior that falls into the grey area. The following diagram results:

Sin and Death: Worse Than We Thought

At this point, there are several things we all need to grasp about sin. First of all, in my opinion, you and I do not sin because we want to make life worse for ourselves. Rather, we sin because we believe it will make life better. We indulge in a negative behavior because we believe it will *improve* our situation. And we perform positive behaviors for the same reason.

Second, anyone or anything from which you and I try to acquire life, value and meaning—outside of the true God—is a false god. Therefore, those positive behaviors aimed at generating life and acceptability for us are sins. So even though *what* we do may be right, the reason *why* we do it is idolatrous.

Third, because you and I lack life and are helpless, no amount of negative *or* positive external behavior is capable of producing an internal transformation.

When my father died, the undertaker did a remarkable job of preparing him for the viewing. He looked incredibly good for someone who wasn't there. Many people whispered to one another in hushed tones, "He looks so alive." But good-looking dead people are still dead. The same is true spiritually. The most a dead, empty, helpless person can do is to turn himself into a more attractive dead person. You'll notice, if you look around, that some people appear less dead and empty than others. But good-looking dead people are still dead—

that is, without any power of their own to produce life within themselves.

2. About the Solution

Now I'd like to complete an illustration I used earlier by labeling the plants that grow out of the soil of shame.

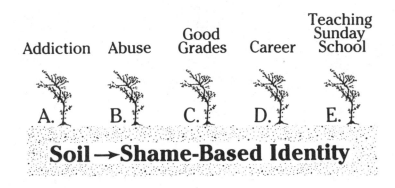

The destructiveness of plants A and B is obvious. They grow out of shame, and their fruits contribute to it. Plants C and D might be those which we are encouraged by society to grow—they're pretty, but tiring. Plant E could be a plant that is nourished by religious pressure to perform. While it might be useful to others, religious performance does nothing to correct the defective soil.

Since the great majority of people with a sense of defectiveness don't know that shame is their problem, they manipulate their outer circumstances or behaviors in order to find inner fulfillment. When all is said and done, the reason why an affair, teaching Sunday school, using drugs, getting good grades, or having possessions doesn't meet people's inner needs is that you can't fix the soil by adjusting the plants; but the plants will eventually change by fixing the soil.

In John 4, we see a picture of Jesus going through Samaria on His way to Galilee. Being tired and hot, He decided to sit by a well and rest. At about noon, a Samaritan woman came to draw water, and Jesus asked her for a drink. This surprised the woman because Jewish males looked down on women and went to great lengths to avoid Samaritans. Let's pick up the conversation in verse 9: ". . . 'How is it that you, a Jew, ask a drink of me, a woman of Samaria?' . . . Jesus answered her, 'If you knew the gift of God, and who it is that is saying to you, "Give me a drink," you would have asked him, and he would have given you living water.' "

Living water? God's gift? We also find out that this woman has had five husbands and is currently living with a man who is not her husband. Sound familiar? What do you think? Do you think this woman hasn't tried hard enough? Try to hear Jesus' next statement, in John 4:13, 14 through the ears of a tired Samaritan woman whose thirst can't be quenched by men, a tired executive whose thirst can't be quenched by women, or a tired Baptist Sunday school teacher whose thirst can't be quenched by her own religious performance: ". . . Every one who drinks of *this* water will thirst again, but whoever drinks of the water that I shall give him will never thirst; the water that I shall give him will become in him a spring of water welling up to eternal life."

Here is the ultimate solution: *living water; the gift of God; that quenches thirst forever!*

How do we tap into that spring of living water? Because of Jesus' death and resurrection, we have a new relationship to sin: "We know that our old self was crucified with him" (Rom. 6:6). We have been made new creations as Paul states: "Therefore, if any one is in Christ, he is a new creation; the old has passed away, behold, the new has come" (2 Cor. 5:17). We no longer need the water from other cisterns that never satisfied, that brought only more thirst and death: "But then what return did you get from the things of which you are now ashamed? The end of those things is death. . . . For the wages of sin is death, but the free gift of God is eternal life in Christ Jesus our Lord" (Rom. 6:21, 23).

What we have now is a very different picture. God's gift on the basis of Christ's performance has transformed an empty, helpless, lifeless enemy of God into a brand new, living creation:

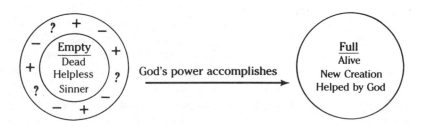

3. About the Enemy

The first thing to remember is that *you are not the enemy!* I have noticed a striking similarity in all shame-based people that I have worked with. They act and think as though they themselves are their own enemy, and they spend incredible amounts of time trying to annihilate self.

It's important at this point to understand some things about our true enemy. First Peter 5:8 says: ". . . Your adversary [enemy] the devil prowls around like a roaring lion, seeking some one to devour." Satan is the enemy of those who get their life from Jesus *and* those who don't.

Further scriptures that reveal the nature of this enemy are: John 8:44: ". . . He was a murderer from the beginning, and has nothing to do with the truth, because there is no truth in him. When he lies, he speaks according to his own nature, for he is a liar and the father of lies." Acts 13:10: He is the ". . . enemy of all righteousness, full of all deceit and villainy . . . making crooked the straight paths of the Lord."

Conning Those Who Lack Life

Perhaps the best passage to illustrate the fact that Satan deceives people who don't know God is 2 Corinthians 4:3, 4: "And even if our gospel is veiled, it is veiled only to those who are perishing. In their case the god of this world has blinded the minds of the unbelievers, to keep them from seeing the light of the gospel of the glory of Christ, who is the likeness of God."

The natural goal of the person who lacks life is to find it. Satan, the liar, offers a counterfeit to those who lack life, by promising them life from a source that can't give it. If that doesn't work, he obscures the seriousness of their condition.

The great con artist's suggestions go something like this: "What you've done is not that bad. *You* are not that bad. You're not dead, and you're not helpless. You are a part-bad/part-good person. You've got some bad qualities and some good qualities. (Doesn't everyone?) So just work on it. Nurture your good side, and deny, ignore, or starve your bad side. You can do it. Just try harder." In short, Satan has the whole world on a self-improvement course. (Remember, people don't sin to make themselves worse.) It looks something like this:

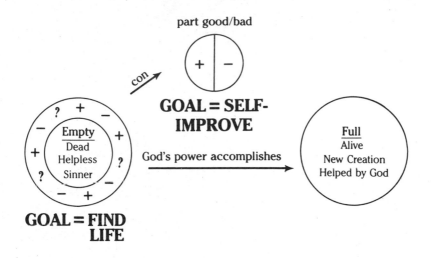

What is the result here? We have someone who is still dead, with a blinded mind, an undersized view of his problem, an oversized view of his ability to fix it, an incorrect view of self, and the wrong goals. If Don and Betty lacked life, they were deceived and were wasting their time.

Conning Those With Life

However, those who lack life are not the only ones to whom Satan lies. He cons those who are alive in Christ too. Revelation 12:10 calls Satan "the accuser of our brethren . . . who accuses them day and night before our God." He uses people, circumstances and memories to condemn us and to obscure the new identity we have as Christians; to deny the completeness of God's work, and to undermine the completely reliable quality of God's love.

The lies are something like this: "God's love is not that certain. God isn't *really* happy with you. You certainly aren't clean, new and alive. You are actually a part-bad/part-good person. You've got some good qualities, which, by the way, you're not supposed to notice or feel too good about. And you've got some bad qualities (but then, who doesn't?), which God wants you to deny, ignore, or starve before He'll be happy with you. So try harder—you can do it!" In short, Satan has a grip on a lot of Christians, who are also on a self-improvement course that looks like this:

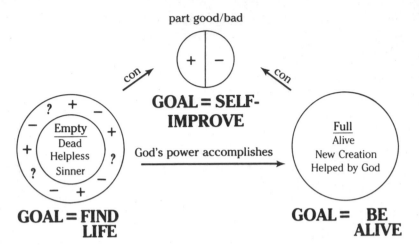

part good/bad

GOAL = SELF-IMPROVE

God's power accomplishes

Empty
Dead
Helpless
Sinner

Full
Alive
New Creation
Helped by God

GOAL = FIND LIFE

GOAL = BE ALIVE

The end result is a Christian who is alive, but who has a blinded mind, an oversized view of the problem, an undersized view of God's solution, and an incorrect view of himself—and the wrong goals. The primary goal of those of us who have been given free life is simply to be as alive as we truly are, and to tell those who lack life where to find it. But Satan has countless Christians living their whole lives trying to earn, with their own behavior, what was already purchased for them by the blood of Jesus: *life, value* and *God's approval*. This is the wrong battle. If Don and Betty *had* life, they were fooled and were surely wasting their time in striving to *find* it.

4. About the Battle

It's ironic how so many Christians can see *this* message as humanistic: "How much money you make is what makes you a valuable, acceptable person." Still, they live as if how much money they *give* is what makes them acceptable. Others condemn Jehovah's Witnesses, Mormons or Muslims for being works-oriented and yet shame one another into supporting programs, teaching classes or building bigger buildings in order to keep God's approval. Still others lift up the cross of Jesus in their songs while acting as if people are second-class spiritual citizens if they don't exercise certain gifts of the Spirit. Those of us who exercise *good* behaviors and avoid bad ones in the name of God look more formidable than others, and we're certainly harder to confront. But the behavior fight is the *wrong* fight.

We are going to learn about and practice fighting the right fight.

These are the two aspects that I believe make up that fight. We are involved in a spiritual battle that will be won through a *fight of faith* and a *renewal of the mind*.

The Fight of Faith

That we are in a spiritual battle at all can be clearly seen in Ephesians 6:10–12: "Finally, be strong in the Lord and in the strength of His might. Put on the whole armor of God, that you may be able to stand against the wiles of the devil. For we are not contending against flesh and blood, but against the principalities, against the powers, against the world rulers of this present darkness, against the spiritual hosts of wickedness in the heavenly places." In 2 Corinthians 10:3, 4, Scripture further describes the nature of our battle: "For though we walk in the flesh, we do not war according to the flesh, for the weapons of our warfare are not of the flesh" (NASB).

We are *not* in a flesh-and-blood battle. We are in a spiritual battle that cannot be won with our own righteous activities. We war against an enemy who wants to destroy us any way he can. Yet, we live as though the accuser of the brethren is going to stop shaming us, and we try to hide from his fiery darts behind our perfect attendance pins or teaching records. The reason Paul tells Timothy to "fight the good fight of faith" (1 Tim. 6:12) is that we are in a real battle, and we are surrounded by forces that would draw us away and promise us life without any power to give it.

Renewing the Mind

In order to fight the right battle, understanding how to renew our mind is equally as important as the faith-fight. Paul says, "Do not be conformed to this world but be transformed by the renewal of your mind . . ." (Rom. 12:2). Notice that he doesn't say, "Be transformed by trying hard to be a good Christian."

This instruction is so simple. "Be transformed," in the Greek, is the same word as *metamorphosis* in English. It means to change from the inside out. But in the Greek it is passive—that is, transformed is something done *to* us, not *by* us. *Transformation is not our job.* It happens as a result of the renewing of our minds.

10

God's Stance Toward the Wounded

Kelli likes God. And she thinks He likes her, too. But this is all kind of new.

Kelli grew up with a dad who traveled a lot, so he was hardly ever there. And since he was an alcoholic, even when he was there he wasn't really there. He called her names, made fun of her, treated her as if she didn't have any right to feel the way she felt or to think what she thought.

He ridiculed her ideas. He treated her as if being a girl were a bad thing. He talked to her and touched her in ways that were disrespectful. He allowed other people to do so, as well. When she tried to tell him how much it hurt her, he acted as if she was the problem for noticing. "That's just the way men are," he said, excusing the hurtful behavior.

To complicate things, during part of Kelli's childhood her dad was a minister. He was hurtful and unfaithful to her mom, and later her parents were divorced. As far as she knew, her dad continued to use women in unhealthy relationships.

Consequently, Kelli learned to perform. She believed that her behavior could control how well her dad survived. And since he didn't survive very well, she felt that it was her fault. She began to push people away. She couldn't trust God. She became self-sufficient, strong and in control—on the outside. On the inside, Kelli felt trapped and out of control.

By the time Kelli grew up and married she was exhausted. She didn't like her marriage, hated herself and wanted to die. When I first saw her, Kelli was suicidal, distrustful, and extremely afraid. I began by giving her the liberty to express her true feelings and to struggle through her pain. I assured her she did not have to perform or look good for me. At the same time, she and her husband had found a church where wounded people didn't have to pretend not to be wounded. They heard that value and acceptance were not earned or protected by religious performance, but were gifts because of Jesus. What was real was more important than how things looked. Kelli began to risk asking for help.

After some time and a lot of work, things are different for Kelli. She still feels cheated, but now she is experiencing a healthy grief for what she never had. She now feels the anger she pretended not to have, but it doesn't control her or get in the way of relationships. She's less afraid. She's learning to trust people, men, her husband—even God. She feels cared for.

Kelli coined a phrase, "The heart-brain barrier." It means knowing a lot of good stuff about God, but not being able to believe it. After much digging, searching, healing and being cared for, the heart-brain barrier has been broken for Kelli. The truth of God's love for her continues to flow from her head to her heart. Kelli likes God. And she thinks He likes her, too.

Learning About the Wrong God

God—What kind of images and feelings does that name bring up in you? Do you want to come closer? Or go in the other direction? Do you sense a liberty to rest? Or do you feel the need to try harder?

My experience with people who struggle with their concept of God is that they are truly in a no-win situation. On one hand, their past experiences with God have typically been very negative, conveying the message that they are defective. They see Him as an uncaring bystander who yawned while they were being abused. And even if He cares, He lacks the power to help. Or, He's a taskmaster—someone to please who cannot be pleased. Or, a deceitful trickster who cannot be trusted. These people have either given up or tried hard, and it has exhausted them.

Noted Christian counselor and author David Seamands says, "Years of experience have taught me that regardless of how much correct doctrine Christians may know, until they have a picture and have felt a sense that God is truly good and gracious, there can be no lasting spiritual victory in their lives."[1] It's time to meet the true God.

---

[1]David Seamands, *Healing of Memories* (Wheaton: Victor Books, 1985), 95.

I want to present to you some pictures of God. Think about them. Struggle with them, if you will. Just allow the possibility that, just maybe, God has gotten some bad publicity by people who falsely represented Him. Perhaps the time has come to renew your mind concerning God. The real God gladly volunteers to be a gracious new source of identity, value and acceptance for all those who ask.

Wounded One . . . Meet God

The idea of a God in heaven who is kind, loving and involved with people is difficult for many people to embrace because of the flesh-and-blood experiences with their fathers or mothers and others in care-giver roles. Real life meant that those who were supposed to be closest were absent, and if they were present they were apathetic or abusive. These experiences have deeply ingrained many memories, beliefs and feelings that easily transfer to the ultimate Care-giver. A lot of people arrive at this conclusion: "If that's what real care-givers are about, God is a phony." My hope is that you'll be able to cross your own heart-brain barrier. By renewing your mind, you'll be able to come to a different diagnosis of the situation: "If that's what the *real* God is like, my care-givers were phonies."

In the *New Testament* there are three distinct roles in which God relates to people: as Father, Son and Holy Spirit. I'd like to spend some time talking about how God relates to wounded, broken people in each of these roles. First, allow me to introduce you to God, our Father.

Let me clarify something at this point. Even if your father and mother never gave you the sense that you were defective, you will most likely have a partially false view or an incomplete view of God. Though you may have *had* a good father, or even now *are* a good father, you still need to know about the *best* Father there is.

God's Stance as Father

Jesus says, "God is spirit" (John 4:24). In Genesis 1, we read that man was created in the image of God, but to truly represent God, He created them male and female. Male and female, however, are flesh-and-blood categories. God is neither man nor woman. And even though Psalms 18:2, 19:14, and 31:3 refer to Him as a rock, God is spirit.

Writers of the Scriptures used male designations and pronouns to describe God, because in the communities which provide the setting for the various parts of the Bible, "maleness" was where all the power, authority and credibility were concentrated. In order for the writers to portray God with all of the authority and power He really does have, they used male terms.

Father, then, refers to God's nature as our Source. He is the Father-Creator; we are His created children.

For those of us who are Christians, however, the fact that God is our Father is even more important. We're alive physically because at one point in time our physical father planted a physical seed. We're alive spiritually because at one point in time our Father, through His Spirit, planted a spiritual seed. "That which is born of the flesh is flesh, and that which is born of the Spirit is spirit" (John 3:6).

There's a difference, however, between the two seeds. Look at 1 Peter 1:23: "You have been born anew, not of perishable seed but of imperishable, through the living and abiding word of God." Born again! A new creation; a brand new person. And the new life that you have is indestructible, which is necessary, because 1 Corinthians 15:50 says: "I tell you this, brethren: flesh and blood cannot inherit the kingdom of God, nor does the perishable inherit the imperishable." Everyone needs a brand new life and identity, and some of us already have it. Everyone needs a new Father, and some of us now have one.

Our heavenly Father begat us; His life and nature is in us: "By which he has granted to us His precious and very great promises, that through these you may escape from the corruption that is in the world because of passion, and become partakers of the divine nature" (2 Peter 1:4).

Our eyes, hair, voice and height were determined by the genes we inherited from our natural parents. In a similar way, the spiritual "gene-pool" from which you and I get our characteristics is that of the Father of all creation. He is our Father!

He Likes Us

Our physical fathers planted a seed that resulted in a child. However, the response of some fathers to the fact that a seed was planted is, "Oh-no!" Some children are unwanted. Have you ever felt unwanted? Ever felt that you were stamped "not good enough" as a person by your father or mother? Ever felt "put-up-with"? God did something more than simply plant a spiritual seed. He wants you. He loves *you*—and He *likes* you!

As a kid I could throw a baseball a mile. Unfortunately, I couldn't throw it *straight*. And I couldn't field the ball very well, either. Some of the most painful, humiliating experiences I remember from childhood are the times when I either was *not* chosen for a team, or I was the *last* one chosen. But "He [the Father] chose us in him before the foundation of the world" (Eph. 1:4). Before the One who created *everything* there is created *anything*, He chose you and me.

You and I were God's first priority. Colossians 3:12 refers to us as "God's chosen ones, holy and beloved. . . ." Peter, in the second chapter of his first epistle, calls us a "chosen race." We all know the pain of not being wanted by someone; not being chosen by those to whom we are closest hurts even more. But you and I *are* wanted. We belong! We've been chosen, handpicked, first team, by our new Father.

Romans 5:6, 8 says, "While we were yet helpless . . . Christ died for the ungodly . . . While we were yet sinners Christ died for us." He didn't wait until we cleaned up our act. He didn't ask for references. Romans 8:15, 16: "For you did not receive the spirit of slavery to fall back into fear, but you have received the spirit of sonship. When we cry, 'Abba! Father!' it is the Spirit himself bearing witness with our spirit that we are children of God." "Abba" means daddy, and father (*pater* in the Greek) means papa, the same word as in the Lord's Prayer. It's "Daddy, Papa," not "Scary Judge."

He chose you. He went through a lot to get you. And now you are His child. He is your dad. And He likes you a lot!

It's Okay to Tell Him Our Pain

Our heavenly Father is not just putting up with us. He likes it when we come around. Hebrews 4:16: "Let us then *with confidence* draw near to the throne of grace, that we may receive mercy and find grace to help in time of need."

We aren't bothering Him with our problems. He isn't going to shame us for not having it all together. He isn't going to give us some formula to perform so we can get back on His good side. He wants to embrace us with grace and mercy when we draw near. Psalms 34:15 says: "The eyes of the Lord are toward the righteous, and his ears toward their cry."

In Christian circles we sometimes have what we call "testimony time," during which people share what God has been doing for them. Have you ever noticed that people hardly ever share pain or struggles? Or if they do, it's always in the past tense, never right now. Not performing doesn't go over very well in religious places. But look at

2 Corinthians 7:5, 6: "For even when we came into Macedonia our flesh had no rest, but we were afflicted on every side: conflicts without, fears within. But God, who comforts the depressed, comforted us . . ." (NASB).

Many Christians would have said, "Fighting without; confidence within," because we've been taught that it isn't acceptable or spiritual to struggle with problems. But notice that Paul says there's trouble on the outside *and* trouble on the inside. Notice, too, that God's response toward those in pain is comfort, not shame for being so human that we have problems.

He's Anxious to Forgive

There's a story in Luke 15 in which Jesus tells about a man who had two sons. The younger one decided he wanted to seek his fortune in the world. So he asked his father for his rightful share of the estate. With his loot in hand, he took off to a distant land. But things started to go wrong. A severe famine hit, and since he had wasted everything he had, he was in big trouble. So he got a job feeding pigs, and eventually ended up struggling with the pigs for their food!

After a while, he figured out that this wasn't working, so he decided to go home. But he was so full of shame he decided that when he got home he would say, "Look, just make me a hired hand, because I'm not *worthy to be a son* any longer."

But as he was coming up the path toward home, his father spotted him (because he had been watching for him) and ran out to meet him. The father hugged and kissed his son again and again. Well, the son said his speech. But the son had never been the son because he was worthy. He was the son because the father was the father. So the father's reaction was to order his servants to bring out the best robe, a ring, and some sandals and put them on his son. Then he ordered the best calf killed, and a huge party commenced for all in the house. "This son of mine was dead," said the father, "but he has come to life again. He was lost and has been found!"

This parable is called the story of the prodigal son. But really it's the picture of a father—*our* Father!—who loves us, who misses us, and responds to our return with an embrace and great joy, as though we had never been away. When you and I are tired and broken from being away from home and we return to our Father, it is as though all heaven throws a party!

He Gives Us His "Yes"

I have a friend I'll call Cheryl whose father always thought her friends were great. He always laughed at their jokes. He was always interested in their accomplishments. His stance toward her friends was *yes*. But toward Cheryl it was *no*. There was no interest, no time, no empathy, no compassion—to him she was not good enough.

But Cheryl has a Father whose stance toward her is *YES*, and she doesn't have to *do* anything to earn His approval. There's nothing she *can* do to get a bigger yes, and there's nothing she can do to get a smaller yes. God's response isn't dependent on what she does. It's about what He did through His Son. It's a free gift. Paul says, "Giving thanks to the Father, who has qualified us to share in the inheritance of the saints in light" (Col. 1:12). Who qualifies us? Our Father.

His Name Is At Stake

During biblical times, a person's name was really important. People gave their babies names that described the characteristics they wanted them to have when they grew up. A name wasn't just a label; it was a description of the *nature* or *character* of the one to whom it belonged. Look at some of God's names:

Elohim, the Strong One;
El-roi, the Strong One who sees;
Jehovah-jireh, He is our Provider;
Jehovah-raffa, He is our Healer;
Jehovah-nissi, He is our Banner;
Jehovah-ra'ah, He is our Shepherd;
Jehovah-shalom, He is our Peace;
Jehovah-tsidkenu, He is our Righteousness;
Jehovah-shammah, He is Present.

These names don't merely describe the ways in which God acts. He does provide, heal, go before us, give us peace, make us righteous. But these are His *Names*; they tell us about His *nature*.

There are many more names of God that aren't listed here, but there is one I want to emphasize—Immanuel. It means "God is with us"; Jesus.

God's Stance as the Son

Luke 4:17–21 says: "And there was given to him [Jesus] the book of the prophet Isaiah. He opened the book and found the place where it was written, 'The Spirit of the Lord is upon me, because he has anointed me to preach good news to the poor. He has sent me to proclaim release to the captives and recovering of sight to the blind, to set at liberty those who are oppressed, to proclaim the acceptable year of the Lord.' And he closed the book . . . and he began to say to them, 'Today this scripture has been fulfilled in your hearing.' "

Do you want to know what Jesus came to do? You have just read His job description. He didn't come for well people, for those who were satisfied, for those who didn't have needs. Jesus came for the poor, the captives, the blind, the oppressed and those who needed forgiveness.

His Compassion

Jesus' compassion went out to the distressed and oppressed: "Then Jesus called his disciples to him and said, 'I have compassion on the crowd, because they have been with me now three days, and have nothing to eat . . .' " (Matt. 15:32).

The word compassion carries with it some extremely deep connotations. It is a mixture of love, anger and grief. Seeing people's needs, their hunger, their pain, their abuse, He felt compassion. When you put the God of the universe in a human body and show Him the pain people are in, how they're abused and placed under burdens they can't carry, His whole being wrenches with compassion.

Jesus' response was never to shame people. He was not disgusted with them. He didn't feel spiritually superior or give tired people some formula to follow. Jesus' compassion toward people in pain always resulted in acting on their behalf—feeding them, healing them, comforting them, meeting whatever need they had.

His Teaching

In Matthew 4:23, we read about Jesus beginning His ministry in Galilee: "And he went about all Galilee, teaching in their synagogues and preaching the gospel of the kingdom and healing every disease and every infirmity among the people."

As you can imagine, news about Him spread, and He became very popular. Soon, an incredibly huge crowd of people was following Him. (If this had happened in our day, the local seminary would have sent their church-growth expert over to see what was happening, so they could franchise it.)

Then Jesus began to say some things that were quite radical—even unpopular. I can see the crowd now. Prostitutes, adulterers, Samaritans, Gentiles, tax-gatherers, the demonized, lepers and other sick people—along with the religious leaders who were interested, the scribes and Pharisees.

What Jesus said came as good news to some and bad news to others: "Blessed are the poor in spirit, for theirs is the kingdom of heaven" (Matt. 5:3). In that crowd there were the broken, tired, poor in spirit. They were *being* shamed and *feeling* shamed for not having it together as well as the religious elite. There were also the self-righteous Pharisees—their opinion of themselves was that they did everything *right*. They didn't need to be broken. They stood to the side and thanked God that they weren't like those depressing, broken people over there. Brokenness doesn't look good; it isn't spiritual.

But Jesus was saying to them all, "Look, you don't understand. The poor in spirit, the broken, are the blessed. It's okay to be broken and tired, because the kingdom comes to such as these."

There are about nine Greek words for mourn in the New Testament alone. In Matthew 5:4: "Blessed are those who mourn, for they shall be comforted," *mourn* means "an outward show of inside pain." To the people who grieve and are broken—so broken that they can't hide it—Jesus is saying: "You're allowed to mourn. It's okay to appear as hurt and wounded and empty as you really are. My comfort is for those who mourn. *Blessed* are those who mourn." To the self-righteous (the religious performers who wouldn't dream of revealing all their "unspiritual" needs and feelings), Jesus is saying: "You don't understand. It's those who mourn that are blessed. 'Well' people don't need comfort. Comfort is for the grieving, the broken."

Jesus says in Matthew 5:27, 28: "You have heard that it was said, 'You shall not commit adultery.' But I say to you, that every one who looks at a woman lustfully has already committed adultery with her already in his heart." And in verses 29, 30: "If your right eye causes you to sin, pluck it out and throw it away; . . . if your right hand causes you to sin, cut it off. . . ."

What in the world is He saying? Remember the audience.

Jesus is talking to the broken and wounded, the sick and the sinners—and to the cream of the religious performers, who measure themselves by themselves and come out okay. On the one hand, there were the adulterers; on the other, there were those who believed that God liked them better because of how chaste they were. They might lust a little, but no big deal. They wouldn't dream of committing adultery.

Can you understand *how* the things Jesus said must have sounded to those two groups? "You broken, wounded, unfaithful adulterers. You need help and you can't help yourselves. You need forgiveness, and you need God to do something for you. You need a new heart.

"And you Pharisees need help, too. You might be rejoicing in how law-abiding and righteous you are, but you are as guilty of breaking the Law as the adulterers are. If you find yourselves looking at a woman lustfully, pluck your eyes out. If you find yourselves touching a woman you shouldn't be touching, cut your hand off. You're in exactly the same shape as the adulterers. You just look better. And after you've done the plucking and cutting, you still have a problem that you can't do a thing about. You need a new heart."

The solution for each of us is full dependence upon Jesus, and receiving what He offers: rest, righteousness, comfort, His kingdom.

If the present relationships that are supposed to represent Jesus in your life don't offer what He offered, don't stop looking until you find new ones that do!

The Son Did It All on the Cross

Ephesians 2:8, 9 says: "For by grace [freely] you have been saved through faith; and this is not your own doing, it is the gift of God—not because of works [what we do], lest any man should boast."

And the next verse says: "For we are his workmanship. . . ." The person who pays for our sins and gives us a gift-based identity is Jesus.

Hebrews 10:10 tells us that by the sacrifice of Jesus, the Son of God, made on our behalf, we have been "sanctified," made holy, *once and for all*. Verse 14 says that He has perfected *"for all time"* those who are sanctified. And in verse 12 we read, "But when Christ had offered for all time a single sacrifice for sins, he sat down at the right hand of God [the Father]."

In the *Old Testament,* the sacrifices of the priests were *never* enough. They could never rest, because the sacrifices had to be repeated time after time—and that's how a lot of us present-day Christians live, isn't it? Jesus, our great high priest, made the sacrifice and sat down. In Acts 7, the account of Stephen's stoning for confronting the religious leaders is given. In verse 55 it says: "But he, [Stephen] full of the Holy Spirit, gazed into heaven and saw the glory of God, and Jesus *standing* at the right hand of God." When it came to making the sacrifice once and for all, to securing our holiness and completeness, Jesus sat down when the work was finished. But when one of those He loves is in trouble or is in pain, He *stands* on their behalf. What a Savior!

God's Stance as the Spirit

When someone becomes a Christian, he receives the indwelling Spirit of God. Galatians 4:6 says: "And because you are sons [and daughters], God has sent the Spirit of His Son into our hearts. . . ." I've already alluded to some of the ways the Spirit of God relates to people, most notably by causing our rebirth described in John 3:3–6. Something else we can know because we have the Spirit is that we are not alone.

Remember the names of God—*El-roi*, the Strong One who sees, and *Jehovah-shammah*, He is Present. Psalms 139:7 says: "Whither shall I go from thy Spirit? Or whither shall I flee from thy presence?" Hebrews 13:5b declares: "I will never fail you nor forsake you."

The Spirit of God is also our Helper. On the eve before His death, Jesus said, "And I will pray the Father, and He will give you another Counselor [Helper, some versions have it], to be with you for ever . . . I will not leave you desolate . . ." (John 14:16, 18). The word "helper" in the Greek is *Paracletos,* which means "the one called along side to help." God's Spirit is inside of us, with us, and along side of us.

While there are many more things that could be said about the Holy Spirit, we will close this chapter with one last description. Let's look at the following verses: "He has put his seal upon us and given us his Spirit in our hearts as a guarantee" (2 Cor. 1:22); "He who has prepared us for this very thing is God, who has given us the Spirit as a guarantee" (2 Cor. 5:5); "You also, who . . . have believed in him, were sealed with the promised Holy Spirit, which is the guarantee of our inheritance. . ." (Eph. 1:13, 14).

The Greek word for "pledge" or "guarantee" in those verses is *arrabon.* It means "engagement ring." The Spirit is God's guarantee, His divine engagement ring which says that you and I are His and He is ours. He is going to return for us someday, but in the meantime, we are sealed in Him. No one else can have us!

For people who feel defective and unwanted at the root of their soul, there is a new truth: God *wants* you. Our identity as children of God is a settled issue. And now that we know we are His, we can also trust Him to resolve the lingering sense of shame that still troubles some of us—long after we have opened our hearts to Him. For God not only "says" we are free of shame, He has made a way for us to escape its deadly grip.

11

God's Solution to Shame: A New Creation

"It's like there are two people inside of me—it's like a civil war. And the more I try to win it, the more I go in circles."

"The goal of most of my Christian life has been this: to become disgusted enough with myself to try hard enough, so that I can finally win God's approval."

"I always thought that in order to do what God liked, I had to do what I hated."

"I thought if I could just hate myself enough, ignore my feelings and drives, that God would finally like me."

These, and statements like them, characterize the lives of tired Christians who don't know *who* they are. The truth, as we've seen, is that the Christian life is a process of *learning to live consistently with who we already are in Christ.* Yet many Christians spend their entire existence unsuccessfully trying to be someone other than who they really are—"for God."

A Christian is a person who has become someone he was not before.[1] The gospel's Good News is that, on the basis of God's grace and because of Christ's performance on the cross, we are *brand new creations.*

Unfortunately, I'm not aware of too many Christians who have experienced the three truths contained in that last statement. While we pay lip-service to the idea that we're accepted because of God's grace, the struggle for acceptance on the basis of works is epidemic. Likewise, we focus on the performance of Christ on the cross as the foundation of our standing with God. Yet, practically speaking, the

---

[1]Needham, *Birthright*, 47.

sermons, books and seminars seem to keep getting back to our performance. But the greatest travesty of all, in my opinion, is the lack of understanding about our new identity in Christ.

It would be disastrous enough if the reason people didn't understand who they are was simply for a lack of information. And the truth is that there *is* an absence of teaching concerning our new identity and what it means to be new creations in Christ. But what is worse, there are volumes of teaching—indeed, entire theologies have developed—that deny, contradict, twist and thereby pervert the Good News concerning our new identity.

Of all the chapters in this book, this one is the most difficult for me to write. The subject is so broad, it encompasses the whole fabric of the Bible. And there are so many theological stances that have come to be regarded as equal to Scripture concerning this subject. I believe, however, this is the most important chapter to grasp in terms of the problem of shame. Understanding what it means to be a new creation is central to your recovery process, because God's solution to shame *is* the new creation.

What *does* the Bible say about those who have a relationship with Jesus? Who *are* we, anyway? And conversely, who are we *not*?

Who We *Are*

Romans 12:1 used to disturb me a lot. I spent most of my Christian life being shamed by it: "I appeal to you therefore, brethren, by the mercies of God, to present your bodies as a living sacrifice, holy and acceptable to God, which is your spiritual worship."

I knew I was to present myself to God, but it seemed that I could never get myself *presentable*. I couldn't quite arrive at the living holy and acceptable. So, instead, I avoided God. Why, with the absence of enough good behaviors and the presence of some negative behaviors, would I want to go near a God who doesn't like us unless our act is together? Being in the condition I was, I was sure God would be very unhappy to get a visit from me.

But then I noticed the word *spiritual*. And I discovered that, literally, it doesn't mean "spiritual" at all, but rather "rational" or "reasonable." In other words, to present my body (self) to God as a living sacrifice, holy and acceptable, was simply rational or reasonable; it meant that I did it with understanding.

Well, I *didn't* understand. Then I read the verse in context—Romans 1 through 11. And God began to show me some other truths in the Bible as well. I discovered that I already *was* alive ("But God, who is rich in mercy . . . made us alive together with Christ." Eph. 2:4, 5). I already *was* made holy ("Therefore, holy brethren, who share in a heavenly call, consider Jesus . . ." Heb. 3:1). I already *was* acceptable because of what God himself did ("Giving thanks to the Father, who has qualified us . . ." Col. 1:12). A paraphrase of Romans 12:1, 2, then, would go something like:

> As a result of the mercy you have received from God, the only thing that makes sense for you to do (someone as alive, and holy and acceptable as you are) is to present yourself to God that way.

The problem was not with God. He wanted me to come near. He welcomed me. In fact, He had already done everything necessary for me to be in close relationship with Him. The problem was that I had no idea of *who* I was and what was true about me because of what He had done.

Let me show you some of the things I found out about *us*. First, I want to show you verses that describe us, because of what God has done. Second, I'll paint a scriptural picture of our new identity. Both demonstrate God's gift-based remedy to our defectiveness.

True Things That Apply to You and Me

Romans 5:1: "Therefore, since we are justified by faith, we have peace with God. . . ." This means that having once and for all been made right by God, being righteous in Him right now, we are completely at peace with God.

5:10: "For if while we were enemies we were reconciled to God. . . ." This means that we have once and for all been restored to a harmonious relationship with God.

6:2: ". . . How can we who died to sin still live in it." Missing the mark has once and for all ceased to be the issue between us and God.

6:11: "So you also must consider yourselves dead to sin and alive to God in Christ Jesus." Not measuring up is never our issue again.

6:14: "For sin will have no dominion over you, since you are not under law but under grace." You are presently not governed by Law but by grace.

7:6: "But now we have been discharged from the Law, dead to that which held us captive, so that we serve not under the old written code but in the new life of the Spirit." We have once and for all been set free from the demands of the Law.

8:1: "There is therefore now no condemnation for those who are in Christ Jesus." We are not at any time under indictment.

1 Corinthians 1:2: ". . . those sanctified in Christ Jesus, called to be saints together with all those who in every place call on the name of our Lord Jesus Christ. . . ." Having been made holy, we have a place with all the saints who have gone before us.

1:5: ". . . in every way you were enriched in him. . . ." Because of Jesus, you and I are a treasure to God, right now.

2 Corinthians 2:15: "For we are the aroma of Christ to God." We are as a sweet-smelling offering to God through Jesus.

Galatians 3:27: "For as many of you as were baptized into Christ have put on Christ." If we have confessed Christ as our Savior, we have his righteousness.

Ephesians 1:3: "Blessed be the God and Father . . . who has blessed us in Christ with every spiritual blessing. . . ." You and I have received every spiritual blessing through Christ.

1:4: ". . . he chose us in Him before the foundation of the world, that we should be holy and blameless before him." His choosing us *then* makes us holy and blameless *now*.

1:6: ". . . to the praise of his glorious grace which he freely bestowed on us in the Beloved." He freely pardoned us because of Jesus.

1:7: "In him we have redemption through his blood, the forgiveness of our trespasses. . . ." We are fully forgiven because of the blood of Jesus.

1:11: ". . . we have obtained an inheritance." We have once and for all been given what is ours because we are His.

2:4, 5: "But God, who is rich in mercy, out of the great love with which He loved us . . . made us alive together with Christ (by grace you have been saved)." God, at all times being merciful, and having once and for all loved us with His great love, has made us alive once and for all, and none of this by our own merit.

Philippians 1:11: ". . . filled with the fruits of righteousness which come through Jesus Christ." You and I are, right now, filled with righteousness through Jesus.

Colossians 1:13: "He has delivered us from the dominion of darkness and transferred us to the kingdom of his beloved Son. . . ." He personally removed us from the authority of darkness and set us in Jesus' kingdom.

2:7: ". . . rooted and built up in him and established in the faith. . . ." We are established in our faith because we are rooted in Jesus.

2:10: ". . . and you have come to fulness of life in him, who is the head of all rule and authority." We are complete and secure in Him. Nothing can be added to make us more acceptable to God.

2:14: ". . . having canceled the bond which stood against us with its legal demands; this he set aside, nailing it to the cross." All of the evidence and charges against us have been cancelled and God's justice has been satisfied.

Hebrews 10:14: "For by a single offering he has perfected for all time those who are sanctified." At one point in time He made us His perfect holy ones, and we will continue to experience the effects of being made perfect.

1 John 1:7: ". . . if we walk in the light, as he is in the light, we have fellowship with one another, and the blood of Jesus His Son cleanses us from all sin." We are called to shamelessly walk in the light of God's love and in fellowship with others, and Jesus' blood continues to cleanse us from our sins.

2:1: ". . . we have an advocate with the Father, Jesus Christ the righteous." At all times, Jesus is on our side, and He is a good defender!

If you are a Christian, the above all applies to you right now. Next we will look at our identity in Christ.

Who We Are

Romans 6:6: ". . . our old self was crucified with him so that the sinful body might be destroyed, and we might no longer be enslaved to sin." We are not who we *used to be*. Our old self was destroyed when Christ died.

8:16: ". . . we are children of God." We belong to His family!

2 Corinthians 5:17: "Therefore, if any one is in Christ, he is a new creation; the old is passed away, behold the new has come." The secret of triumph over our past is the creation that we are in Christ.

Galatians 3:29: ". . . heirs according to promise." Everything He has is ours.

Ephesians 2:10: "For we are his workmanship, created in Christ Jesus for good works, which God prepared beforehand, that we should walk in them." He created us and sustains us in a walk prepared and planned before we were born.

Colossians 1:22: ". . . he has now reconciled [you] in his body of flesh by his death, in order to present you holy and blameless and irreproachable before him." By His death we are made to be without blame. We are *not* a reproach to God.

Hebrews 3:1: ". . . holy brethren, who share in a heavenly call." As holy ones, we are *wholly* included in God's plan.

1 Peter 1:23: "You have been born anew, not of perishable seed but of imperishable. . . ." We are born of a good seed that will never die.

2:9: "But you are a chosen race, a royal priesthood, a holy nation." We have been specially selected and belong to royalty.

2 Peter 1:4: ". . . partakers of the divine nature." His nature is our nature.

As you can readily see, our identity is not based upon our performance. The above are simply true statements that describe the new creation that you are in Christ. The Christian life is *not* an exercise in positive self-effort stemming from a negative self-concept (in the name of God). It's learning to live by faith in a way that is consistent with who we already are and what we already have because of the performance of a God who is faithful.

Who We Are Not

Remember who you were? Dead, empty, helpless, lost, condemned. You were an enemy of God, and very tired. But by the love of the Father, the action of the Son, and the power of the Spirit, God has made you into a new creation. It's a free gift.

Unfortunately, there are some prevalent beliefs, even *doctrines*, that pervert the truth about our new identity in Christ. They are as harmful as they are widespread. They place the burden of victory in life on positive human performance (which always results in shame or self-righteousness). At the same time that they demand holiness, these beliefs make excuses for falling short. The bad news is that there *is* no excuse for falling short. The Good News is that there *is* forgiveness and cleansing. The rest of this chapter is dedicated to countering beliefs that are widely accepted theologically, but are not scripturally sound and true.

The Sin Nature

"Sin nature" is a phrase used to describe the fallen nature that we inherited from the first man, Adam, as a result of the Fall. It is a view that has been accepted in the church for centuries. It probably began to be propagated in A.D. 300–400, around the time of the famous church father, St. Augustine.

The view states that the sin nature results from our being the offspring of Adam, the first sinner. Probably one of the hallmark texts used to promote this idea is Romans 5:12: "Therefore as sin came into the world through one man, and death through sin, and so death spread to all men, because all men sinned."

Included in this approach are various associations between the sin nature and our humanity, our bodies, our selves, or "the flesh." Having a sin nature and being in the flesh are equated as being one and the same. Texts used to support the idea of a great battle between God's Spirit and our sinful nature are Romans 7 and 8, as well as Galatians 5 and 6. And the teaching says that we will be stuck with the sin nature until we die.

The phrase, however, is a theological one and not truly scriptural. The error comes with the various translations of the words "self," "man," "flesh"—as nature. The view that man has a sin nature dramatically minimizes his *true* problem. Man's problem is not what he has; it is what he is—and that is *dead*. In other words, he doesn't have life. Look at Romans 5:12 again: "Sin nature" is not even mentioned in the verse. Something *worse* than a sin nature has spread. And that is death. The man's problem who is outside of Christ is not what he has; it is who he is. And who he is can be changed only by God.

The phrase "death spread to all men, because all men sinned" is the key. First, death is what was passed on, not an evil nature. Secondly, *all* missed the mark—*all* were dead. Romans 3:23 says, ". . . for all have sinned and fall short of the glory of God." And what sin earns is death.

Use of the phrase "sin nature" is common in the theological explanations of countless books, sermons and devotionals. It is also notable in several popular translations of the Bible. That the sin nature and the flesh are viewed as one and the same thing can be seen in the fact that some translate flesh (from the Greek) as sin nature. This is not telling the reader what the text *says* in the original. It is giving the reader a theological interpretation.

128

Old Nature/New Nature

I remember going to Sunday school as a child and hearing my teacher tell a story which was his attempt at describing the battle of the Christian life: "An old Indian chief had two dogs, a black one and a white one. They used to fight all the time, and the one he fed was the one that always won. So he always made sure he fed the one he wanted to win."

So goes the doctrine of the two natures: "Outside of a relationship with God, we have a sin nature. It is also called the 'old self,' the 'old man,' or the 'old nature.' After we come into a relationship with God, through Christ, we are given a new additional nature. It is also called the 'new self' or 'new man.' This means that after we become a Christian, we have two natures coexisting within us.

"However, they don't get along very well. The victory in the Christian life depends, then, on how well we are able to starve, ignore, or deny the old self, and how well we feed the new self. The war is within us, between our two selves, one good and one bad." Does this explanation sound familiar? It's Satan's "con." And the proof given that the old nature is still there is the fact that we still sin.

Personally, I have some problems with this teaching. First of all, the position is built from the beginning on the wrong assumption or emphasis that man *has* an old nature, as opposed to *being* dead. Like the doctrine of a sin nature, this doctrine of two natures residing in us is not scriptural. While there are references to the old self, as well as allusions to old and new directions, the term "old nature" is not found, unless self or man has been incorrectly translated "nature." Likewise, there is no place in the Bible that talks about the old and new natures ever existing at the same time, let alone being at war with each other. The battle is not between two me's. I am not at war with the Spirit of God either. The struggle in the Christian life is that of choosing whether to walk by the Spirit or by the flesh. We'll discuss more about this battle in the next chapter.

Notice too that "self" carries the connotation of a complete being, while "nature" seems to indicate aspects or parts of being.[2] Romans 6:6 says: "We know that our old self [man] was crucified with him." It is a once-and-for-all completed action, something done *to* you and not *by* you. The old self can no more be recrucified than Christ can be, and even if it could be, *you couldn't do it.*

John 3:3, 6 is a strong argument against the old nature/new nature

---

[2]John Murray, *The Epistle to the Romans* (Grand Rapids: Eerdmans, 1968), 219.

idea. In this passage Jesus says: ". . . unless one is born anew, he cannot see the kingdom of God . . . That which is born of the flesh is flesh, and that which is born of the Spirit is spirit."

When each of us was conceived physically, a new creation came to life that did not exist before. When someone is born again, of the Spirit, a new creation comes to life that did not exist before. Our old selves cannot see the kingdom of God. Only new creations can see heaven.

To further illustrate the point, let's look at 2 Corinthians 5:17. Here, the Apostle Paul says: "Therefore if any man is in Christ, he is a new creation; the old has passed away; behold, the new has come." The most literal Greek-to-English rendering of this is:

> If anyone is in Christ, that one is a new creation; at one point in time the old things completely passed away; behold, at one point in time the new things came to be; we have experienced the continuing effects of that, and we will continue to experience them.

A new creation is something that wasn't there before. Notice, too, that Paul doesn't say, "If anyone is in Christ, he is a part old/part new creation; the old is partially passed away, and some new things have come." I am convinced that if this was an accurate description of the new Christian's condition, Paul would have said so.

To sum up what we have said, it is a mistake to think of the believer as consisting of both an old and a new man or as having in him both an old and a new nature.[3] The old man is the unregenerate man; the new man is the regenerate man created in Christ unto good works. It is no more feasible to call a believer a new man and an old man, than it is to call him a regenerate man and an unregenerate.[4] The old man ceased to exist at the time of our regeneration.[5]

Death to Self

The "death to self" teaching comes mainly from the interpretation of two passages of Scripture. The first is Galatians 2:20, which says: "I have been crucified with Christ; it is no longer I who live, but Christ lives in me; and the life I now live in the flesh I live by faith in the

[3]John Murray, *Principles of Conduct; Aspects of Biblical Ethics* (Grand Rapids: Eerdmans, 1957), 218.

[4]W.H. Griffith-Thomas, *St. Paul's Epistle to the Romans* (Grand Rapids: Eerdmans, 1946), 168.

[5]David Seamands, *Healing for Damaged Emotions*, (Wheaton: Victor Books, 1981), 73.

Son of God, who loved me, and gave himself for me." The second is a comment Paul makes in 1 Corinthians 15:31: "I die every day."

This approach to the Christian life revolves around denying self, which usually includes, but is not limited to, our feelings, drives, needs and likes. It says that every time one of those "unspiritual" human elements raises its ugly head, we are supposed to look at it in disgust and shame it out of existence. In order to do what God wants, you have to do what you don't want. If you like something, it is probably wrong or selfish.

The problem with this approach is that it misinterprets Galatians 2 and takes 1 Corinthians 15 out of context. The phrase "have been crucified" in Galatians 2:20 means that at one point in time, I was crucified. It is something that was done *to* me and not *by* me. Notice, also, that even after being crucified with Christ, and even after Christ is living in me, there is still "the life I *now live*." A brand new "I"? But instead of living by trying hard to annihilate self and do what I hate in an attempt to please God, the life I now live I live *by faith* in the Son of God.

In 1 Corinthians 15, Paul is banking on the fact that the dead are raised up again. It's like he's saying, "If the dead aren't raised up, why am I doing this? Why do I constantly put myself in dangerous situations, and fight with wild animals, and stick my neck out as I do? The dead better be raised up, because I could go any minute. *I die daily!*" As you can see, this phrase has nothing to do with death to self. Paul's life was on the line every day.

On a more practical note, the reason this teaching is totally unhelpful to those who feel a sense of shame in their lives, and to everyone else in general, is that in its effort to deny self, it actually results in focusing *on* self. People who are trying to bring about their own death to self are really preoccupied with self. And they are constantly looking at themselves to make sure they are "dead" enough.

What a tiring way to live!

God's Word

How could a creation be both old and new at the same time? How could a person be both dead and alive at the same time? How could a person be both in darkness and in the light at the same time? We need to start taking what the Bible says about us seriously. We need to start looking at what God did and begin to interpret our experience based on Scripture, instead of looking at ourselves and interpreting Scripture based on our experience.

In His instructions to His people, God says in Exodus 23:7, "Keep far from a false charge, and do not slay the innocent and righteous, for *I will not acquit the wicked*." God is saying that He will not let those who are guilty get by with their wickedness. In order to let someone who was as guilty as we were off the hook, He didn't simply overlook our guiltiness. Jesus paid the penalty for us. He *made* us innocent through His Son.

When God said, "Let there be light" there was light. Why? Because He said it. His Word brought it about. And when God says, "You are new, justified, reconciled, alive, holy and blameless, my children and heirs," we can count on its validity because God made us so through His Word—Jesus. "And the Word became flesh and dwelt among us . . ." (John 1:14).

Conclusion

In John 7:38 Jesus says, "He who believes in me, as the scripture has said, 'Out of his heart shall flow rivers of living water.' " Believing in God's living Word, Jesus, as our Source is how we go from death to life. But practicing hanging on to Him by faith on a day-to-day basis is how to have lives of fullness and freedom. Colossians 2:6 says: "As therefore you received Christ Jesus the Lord, so live in Him." God gave His Son so we might have life, but also that we might "walk in newness of life" (Rom. 6:4).

And "Do not be conformed to this world but be transformed by the renewal of your mind" (Rom. 12:2). Continue to learn about and accept who you already are and what you already have because of Jesus. "And you will know the truth, and the truth will make you free" (John 8:32). Develop the picture of your worth and value from God, not from the false reflections that come out of your past.

It is to this faith fight—the daily business of learning to live out what God declares to be true of us—that we will now turn.

12

Fighting the New Fight: Theologically

One day I was riding in the car with our fourteen-year-old daughter Kara. Out of the corner of my left eye, I caught some movement. There, just barely over the treetops and flying parallel to our car, were two huge Canada geese. I adjusted my foot on the accelerator in order to match their speed. As near as I could tell, they were going a little more than fifty miles per hour. I was amazed. I'd hunted geese for many years, and I knew then why I'd missed so many.

Grabbing Kara's sleeve, I pointed to the geese and said, "Look at how fast those geese are flying. Isn't that incredible?"

"I'll bet they're really tired from flapping their wings," she said matter-of-factly. "If I were ever a bird, I'd want to be one that soars."

I don't think that under normal circumstances geese get tired from flapping their wings. But the depth of Kara's insight into life more than made up for her lack of insight into goose physiology. It also provided me with an insight into my own spirituality. If I had to be a bird, I'd like to be that soaring kind, too. And I'd like to be the kind of Christian that soars instead of flaps, as well. Because when your focus is on performance, you learn to flap really hard.

Isaiah 40:29, 31 says, "He gives power to the faint, and to him who has no might He increases strength . . . but they who wait for the Lord shall renew their strength, they shall mount up with wings like eagles, they shall run and not be weary, they shall walk and not faint." Eagles soar!

Getting Into the Right Fight

If you're a Christian, the old you is dead and you are brand new. It is *not* a battle between your evil nature and God's Spirit, as if you and

God were at odds. Paul says, "Therefore having been justified by faith, we have *peace* with God through our Lord Jesus Christ" (Rom. 5:1, NASB).

The prophet Ezekiel, anticipating the effects of God's Spirit on His people, says: "Then I will sprinkle clean water on you, and you will be clean; I will cleanse you from all your filthiness and from all your idols. Moreover, I will give you a new heart and put a new spirit within you; and I will remove the heart of stone from your flesh and give you a heart of flesh. And I will put My Spirit within you and cause you to walk in My statutes, and you will be careful to observe My ordinances" (Ezek. 36:25–27, NASB).

Did you grasp the promises? First, God says He'll replace our hard hearts with ones that are soft. Second, we will be clean because *He* will make us clean. Third, He will put His Spirit within us and by means of His Spirit, *He* will cause us to be obedient and lawful. God himself will be in charge of our new behavior.

In Philippians there is a verse that rightly describes our task: "Let us keep living by that same standard to which we have attained" (3:16, NASB). Paul urges that we live consistent with the standard we have already attained in Christ, remembering that we haven't achieved it by any effort on our part, but because of Christ's work on the cross.

This chapter and the two that follow are about learning to fight a new fight, to soar consistently on the outside with who we already are on the inside.

The "Flesh"

". . . walk by the Spirit," Paul says in Galatians 5:16, "and you will not carry out the desire of the flesh." Notice that the command is to walk by the Spirit. The *result* of walking by the Spirit will be to *not* carry out the desires of the flesh. This is the essence of the Christian battle. Learning to practice "walking by the Spirit" is really what our part of the Christian life is all about. As Christians, we have the choice to either "walk by the Spirit" or to "walk by the flesh."

First, it's necessary to have a correct understanding of the concept of "flesh" in order to fully appreciate our fight. Forms of the Greek word *sarx* appear numerous times in the New Testament. Translated correctly, it literally means flesh, fleshly, fleshy, or of flesh. Paul uses the concept in several places in Scripture and in a variety of ways. In every instance, there appears to be something "natural" (as opposed to supernatural) about the flesh.

For instance, flesh could simply mean the natural material out of which we are made, as in John 3:6, "That which is born of the flesh is flesh." It could mean our own self-effort, as in Paul's confrontation in Galatians 3:2–5. The Galatians had begun their Christian journey by a supernatural work of the Spirit and were now trying to complete it with their own religious self-effort. Because of that, Paul asked, "Are you now ending [being perfected] by the flesh?" It could refer to the source people draw on for their life, value and meaning. The Corinthians had a supernatural Source in Christ, but they were drawing on natural sources ("I am of Paul, I am of Apollos, I am of Cephas"). In 1 Corinthians 3:1, Paul says, "But I, brethren, could not address you as spiritual men [drawing from your supernatural Source], but as men of the flesh [drawing from what is natural]."

An unfortunate thing has happened, however, as a result of incorrect theology coming through sermons, curriculums, songs, even Bible translations. *Sarx* has come to be understood as something different from its true meaning. It's been interpreted and translated as sinful man, sin nature, unspiritual, or worldly. This interpretation is incorrect and promotes a very limited, even stereotypical notion that the flesh is always and only bad or sinful. Consequently, when we hear the term "flesh," we're left with only a caricature of the meaning. We automatically think of greediness, lustfulness, dirty movies, selfishness, adultery and the like. These are, indeed, things that result from relying on the flesh (what is natural), yet they are not the same as the flesh.

It is clear that no matter how good we become in the flesh (our own self-effort), our attempts to gain God's favor fall short. Romans 3:20 reminds us: "Because by works of the Law no flesh will be justified in His sight" (NASB). It could never be done through our flesh, because our flesh (natural self-effort) is weak. Sin (not measuring up) is an outworking of weakened flesh.

God in the Flesh

But while the flesh is weak, it is not *automatically* sinful. John 1:14 says: "And the Word became flesh, and dwelt among us. . . ." In Jesus, God himself came and dwelt in the flesh—the same form as we are right now. The fact that Jesus was sent in the flesh does not mean that He was sinful. It doesn't mean He had a sinful nature, or that He was unspiritual or worldly. It just means that He existed in a bodily form, like us. Look at the following diagram to get a picture of the situation so far:

	In the flesh (form)		
Jesus	Yes		

However, even though Jesus was *in* the form of flesh while He was on the earth, He was never *of* the flesh as (His source)—that is, at no point did He ever draw His life, acceptance, value, power from what was natural. The flesh was never His Source, even though Satan tempted Him to turn to natural things to meet His needs (Matt. 4). He lived *in* the flesh, but never *of* or *according* to the flesh. He walked according to the Father, meaning that He continued to rely on God (Father and Spirit) as His Source of life: This relationship could be illustrated as follows:

	In the flesh (form)	Of, by, or according to the flesh (source)	Of, by, or according to the Father and Spirit (source)
Jesus	Yes	No	Yes

Before we were Christians, we were not only *in* the flesh (form). "That which is born of the flesh is flesh" (John 3:6). We were also *of* the flesh (source). Fleshly things, those which are natural, were all that we had to choose from for our life. And we tried, unsuccessfully, to get our lives *from* the flesh (natural things: money, sex, power, religion, people's opinions). And even though the flesh didn't deliver, we continued to live according to the flesh on an ongoing basis.

Natural things were our god, our source. We were *in* the flesh and *of* the flesh. It looked something like this:

	In the flesh (form)	*Of, by, or according to the flesh (source)*	*Of, by, or according to the Father and Spirit (source)*
Jesus	Yes	No	Yes
Us without life	Yes	Yes	No

I used to think that a Christian was someone who *gave* his life *to* God. But what life does a dead person have to give to God? In Romans 5, Paul says that before our relationship with Christ, we were dead. Rather, a Christian is someone who *gets* his life *from* God. Ezekiel 37:14 says: "And I will put My Spirit within you, and you shall live. . . ." A person becomes a Christian when he gets his life *from* God. His Spirit is the only source of power that can give life. When we get life from the Spirit at the time of our salvation, that which is natural (the flesh) is no longer our source. Galatians 5:24 says: "And those who belong to Christ Jesus have crucified the flesh with its passions and desires." Obviously this doesn't mean that we are no longer *in* the flesh. A look in the mirror will tell us that. It just means that the flesh, that which is natural, is no longer the source for those who have Jesus as their Source. I've tried to picture it for you:

	In the flesh (form)	*Of, by, or according to the flesh (source)*	*Of, by, or according to the Father and Spirit (source)*
Jesus	Yes	No	Yes
Us without life	Yes	Yes	No
Us with life	Yes	No	Yes

This brings us to what some will call "the battle": "Walk by the Spirit." Paul tells us in Galatians 5:25: "If we live by the Spirit, let us also walk by the Spirit." In other words, if God's Spirit is the Source from which we get our lives, let's continue to live and walk by that Source. We have a supernatural life, from a supernatural Source, even as we live in a natural form, totally surrounded by natural terrain (flesh). Our choice, our struggle, then, is to either walk by the Spirit or to walk by the flesh. Look at the last diagram:

	In the flesh (form)	Of, by, or according to the flesh (source)	Of, by, or according to the Father and Spirit (source)
Jesus	Yes	No	Yes
Us without life	Yes	Yes	No
Us with life	Yes	No	Yes
Us with life (Our struggle)	Yes	Yes/No	Yes/No

The Importance of Renewing Your Mind

By now you might be asking, "Why is this guy spending so much time talking about the "flesh"? Because, if we're going to experience different lives and behaviors that result from fullness in Christ and not from religious self-effort, we need to understand the place of the flesh in our fight to "renew" the mind." In Romans 12:2 it says: "Do not be conformed [squeezed from the outside] to this world, but be transformed [changed from the inside out] by the renewal of your mind." If it were just a matter of changing your mind, it would seem simple, except for one thing.

Paul, in Philippians 3:4, says, "Though I myself have reason for confidence in the flesh [that which is natural] (Paul was a religious zealot before He found Christ): If any other man *thinks* he has reason for confidence in the flesh, I have more." Not only do we live in the flesh (in our physical bodies), we have a mind to put confidence in the flesh. In other words, we are programmed, trained, in the habit of, practiced up at putting confidence in natural things. That's how we think. Living in shame-based relationship systems further teaches people to trust in natural things. Value and acceptance come from what people think, how things look, how well we perform at school, in sports, at our job, or around the relatives. In shame-based religious systems, acceptance by people (and supposedly by God) comes from attending, giving, teaching classes and performing a host of religious activities (also supposedly for God).

Most modern approaches to understanding ourselves and making changes in our lives focus on the central ingredient of effort. Whether our problem is doing something we wish we weren't doing, or wanting to completely surrender our life to God, or struggling to believe God really loves us, the line is still the same: *Try harder!*[1] Let's just ask a question here: Is it possible that people are being shamed in the name of God and taught to walk by the flesh under the guise of spirituality? Yes!

Reintroducing the "Rest Cycle"

So how can we untangle this? Where do we go from here? We're at the point where we need to learn a new cycle to replace the old, tired "give-up/try-hard" way of living. Let's look at the diagram again from chapter 8:

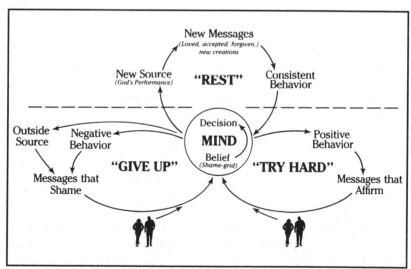

Now that you've seen what "flesh" is, think about the "give-up/try-hard" cycle. Can you see that replacing negative behaviors with

---

[1]Larry Crabb, *Inside Out*, (Colorado Springs, Colo.: Navpress, 1988), 43.

positive behaviors is still walking by the flesh? Even though it is harder to confront, it is still sin. You're still trying to meet your needs, and to get a sense of acceptance and fulfillment from something other than God.

But now you have a new Source and new messages, a totally new place in which to put your confidence. But, you also have a mind (or a habit) to put confidence in the flesh. It's almost as if you *will* put confidence in the flesh "automatically" if you don't choose purposely to rest in God and what He has done. The battle's frontline is in the mind.

In the Philippians 3 passage, where Paul says he has a mind to put confidence in the flesh, he also goes on to list all the reasons why this is so natural for him. If you were a religious person, you'd have a great list too. But Paul urges us, in this passage, to put *no confidence* in the flesh, but rather to "glory in Christ Jesus"!

Fighting the Fight

A few years ago, I wrote an item in our church newsletter about an incident that happened in the church. For one person in particular, the incident was still very fresh. Eventually, I found out through the grapevine that what I said had hurt her. I felt guilty, and I was ashamed that so many other people knew about it. Apologizing to her would have been the right course of action, but I struggled with the prospect. Why? You may ask. Well, inside me there was a "rule" that said, "Good counseling pastors don't say hurtful things to people." If I apologized, I would be admitting that I was wrong, which at that time was very condemning to me. Also, it bothered me that I found out about the offense from others, rather than from the person I had offended. "She didn't follow God's instructions in such a case," I reasoned. "She should have come directly to me." The actual truth was, I was ashamed that others had found out. Besides that, I was concerned that she would reject me if I tried to talk to her.

At this point, I was faced with three alternatives: 1. *To not apologize.* Walking by the flesh (people's opinions, my own need to do everything right, my need for people's approval) would result in no apology.

2. *To simply apologize because it's the right thing to do.* (Despite my personal difficulty with admitting my imperfection and my fear of rejection.) This would be the right choice, because the Law says, "Good Christians (*especially* counseling pastors) always apologize."

And what would people think if I didn't apologize? So I gritted my teeth and did it. Walking by the flesh (people's opinions, my own ability to do the right thing), in this case resulted in the "right" behavior.

3. *Apologize because of who I am through the work of Jesus and His Spirit.* This would have been the best alternative. Regardless of the flesh (her acceptance, people's opinions, my own attempts to be lawful, which in this case *fell short*), I might have decided that what Jesus says about me is the truth. I am totally loved and acceptable as a result of His performance. My value is not up for grabs. If I had walked by the Spirit, drawing life from those truths, I would have been free to apologize, no matter what the response, no matter what my negative or positive behavior seemed to be saying about me. Walking by the Spirit (hanging on to Jesus) would have resulted not only in the right behavior, but it would have resulted in doing it in the right spirit. My relationship with that woman would have been reconciled because of what Jesus did. When we walk in the Spirit we are *free* (like soaring eagles) and the love of Jesus permeates all we do.

Actually, the faith fight I'm talking about is described in *many* different ways by the various writers of Scripture. I've already referred to three ways of describing the choices we make in our new fight: walk by the Spirit, put our confidence in Him, and glory in Christ. Let me show you a picture of how this fight works.

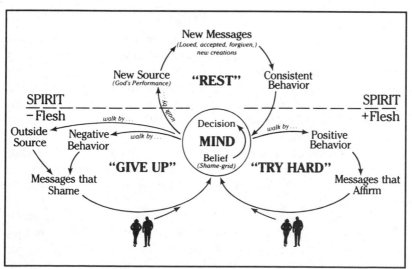

On the one hand, if we choose to fight a behavior battle, we have two alternatives: exercising a negative behavior or a positive behavior. In either case, the resulting messages about us are waiting for and dependent upon *our* performance, whether good or bad. If we fail and give up, we're shamed. If we try hard and succeed, we're self-righteous. God is not satisfied with either one of those outcomes. On the other hand, we can choose to rest in Christ's performance for us. Then the proper behavior becomes an agreement with the truth that we fight to settle in our minds.

Let me describe it still another way. It's almost as if Paul is saying, "Look, everyone glories in something. Don't glory in your own performance. Sometimes it's not that glorious. Don't glory in the fact that you read your Bible every day. You might miss a day. Don't glory in your bank account. We could have a depression. That wouldn't be very glorious. *You* glory in Christ Jesus."

Everybody puts confidence in *something* as his source of life, value, and acceptance. Don't put confidence in your athletic ability. You might get injured, or perform miserably. Don't put confidence in your grades. You might get an *F*. Don't put confidence in people's opinions of you. They might change their minds. *You* put your confidence in Jesus, in what He's done, and in the stability of what that says about you.

More Ways of Describing the Fight

In Philippians 3:1 Paul says, "Finally, my brethren, *rejoice in the Lord*. To write the same things to you is not irksome to me, and is safe [a safeguard] for you." A safeguard against what? For years I thought that rejoicing in the Lord was a safeguard against being sad or depressed. In other words, if you're sad, just "rejoice in the Lord." If you're depressed, "praise God anyway." But examine the context: "Look out for the dogs, look out for the evil workers, look out for those who mutilate the flesh [false circumcision]." Remember them? They were men who followed behind Paul and taught the Christians that faith in what Jesus did wasn't quite enough. They had to get circumcised, too.

The reason "rejoice in the Lord" is a safeguard is that someone was urging the Philippian Christians to rejoice in the fact that they were such good religious performers. But Paul says, "No! Everyone rejoices in something. Some people rejoice in the flesh (what is natural), but *you* rejoice in the Lord! Choose to rejoice in the right thing!"

In 1 Timothy 6:17 Paul says to Timothy, "As for the rich in this world, charge them not to be haughty, nor to set their hopes on uncertain riches but on God who richly furnishes us with everything to enjoy." Notice that this verse is not saying that riches are bad, but that they are uncertain. So *you* fix your hope on something certain, the certainty of God and what He says about you.

Paul says:

> He is the source of your life in Christ Jesus, whom God made our wisdom, our righteousness and sanctification and redemption; therefore, as it is written, "Let him who boasts, boast in the Lord" (1 Cor. 1:30, 31).

Everyone boasts in something. Some people boast in their cars. But cars get old and rust; they're dispensable. Some boast in their homes or other personal possessions. All these can be lost or destroyed; they are of this earth, corruptible. Some boast in family members or friends; people are of the flesh, and can fail us. Some will even boast in the fact that they give a lot of money to the church or to charity. There are plaques or stained-glass windows to acknowledge or praise such offerings, but these too pass away, and people forget. Jesus said these already have their reward in full here on earth. But *you* decide to boast in the Lord and in what He did. In doing so, you choose to base your stability on unshakeable, eternal things.

Ephesians 6:10 says: "Finally, be strong in the Lord, and in the strength of His might." The Greek word for "be strong" literally means "allowing yourself to be strengthened." Some people try to get their strength from people, but we've already said that people can fail us. Some seek strength in drugs or alcohol, but we all know where these lead. Strength is not found in investments and properties. Stocks crash; economies fail. Everyone needs to get strength from something. But *you* get your strength from the only One who is strong—the Lord.

In Ephesians 6:14–16, Paul says: "Stand therefore, having girded your loins with truth, and having put on the breastplate of righteousness, and having shod your feet with the equipment of the gospel of peace; above all taking up the shield of faith, with which you can quench all the flaming darts of the evil one." We all put on some form of protection to keep away shame and judgments. Some people put on smiles. Some people put on a wounded, helpless demeanor. Some put on high-powered careers. Others put on tithing their money, serving on a church committee, or going to the mission field; all of which can be forms of their *own* righteousness. But *you* put on Jesus' righteousness and take up His shield of faith. His righteousness is yours; it's a settled issue. The armor is impenetrable; Satan's darts bounce off of it.

In 1 John 3:6 it says: "No one who abides in Him sins." Wrongly interpreted, this verse sounds enormously indicting. Some people try not to sin simply by *trying not to sin*. Some people try not to sin by abiding in the Law. Some attend Christian formula seminars seeking a way to avoid sin. Literally, the verse says, "No one who is *presently* abiding in Jesus is *presently* sinning." It is impossible for us to both depend on Christ and yet, at the same time, miss the mark by depending on something other than Him. Abide in Him, put your trust in Him, and He will keep you moment by moment from the practice of sin.

Paul says, "Be filled with the Spirit." Literally, this says, "Allow yourself to keep being fulfilled by the Spirit." Everyone tries to be complete, or fulfilled, by someone or something: money, marriage, religion, power, houses or lands. Out of all that could fill up your life, *you* keep getting filled from the one source that truly completes and equips you—the Spirit.

Walking by the Spirit

Growing up in a church, I was taught that walking by the flesh meant going to movies, reading *Playboy* magazines, or dancing. Walking by the Spirit was going to church, reading your Bible and praying. But one of the most incredible awakenings of my life came when I realized what the flesh was for the Galatians. The Galatians were *not* going to movies, reading dirty magazines, or dancing. They were getting circumcised! *Religion was the fleshly indulgence of Galatia!* They were measuring their acceptability by their own religious performance.

Let's go back to the Philippians 3 passage once more. Remember Paul, who chose to put no confidence in the flesh—even though it was great-looking flesh. What brought him to the place where he could do that? He says:

> But whatever gain I had, I counted as loss for the sake of Christ. Indeed, I count everything as loss because of the surpassing worth of knowing Christ Jesus my Lord. For his sake I have suffered the loss of all things, and count them as refuse, in order that I may gain Christ (Phil. 3:7, 8).

What caused him to change his mind? Perhaps God just tapped

Paul on the shoulder one day and said, "Look, Paul, how would you like to leave behind all your status, the respect you have in the religious community, burn all your 'perfect attendance pins' and become a Christian so you can be mistreated the rest of your life and eventually lose your head?" I don't think so. What really happened is that on his way to do more good works in God's name, Paul saw the truth—and it demolished all his good works. God confronted Paul with his need for Jesus. I think the more good works we have going, the harder it is to know, or to remember, that our only hope is God. It's *not* just that "things go better with Jesus." Jesus said, "Apart from Me you can do *nothing*" (John 15:5).

Paul discovered that real life comes from continuing to depend upon, draw life from, receive our value and acceptance from the Spirit. It comes from learning that what is natural, whether *good* or *bad,* is dead and has no real life to offer.

I have no doubt Paul won the fight of faith. And you can, too.

Beginning now.

13

Fighting the New Fight: In Real Life

Recently, I heard about a retreat that was held for the young people and youth workers of a large church in the West. The speakers worked with a parachurch ministry that focused primarily on teenagers in crisis. Their sessions centered on people in pain, the recovery process, and the need for the church to be a safe place in which people can struggle and heal. It was a very refreshing weekend for many who attended.

For one particular youth worker, named Alice, it was a most significant experience. She realized for the first time that health is not just about positive behaviors, and that recovery is a process that takes time. Second, she realized that her church not only neglected to deal with people in pain but actually encouraged people to be dishonest about their struggles.

Alice felt compassion for the "distressed and downcast," just as Jesus did. She was so moved by her new realizations that she decided to do something about it when she got home. She wrote an open letter to the leadership and the congregation, talking about the need to get real with the problems facing individuals and families. She had her most painful experience, however, when she was not allowed to mail the letter and was told not to share her observations because she was "too negative." This was a repeat performance of what happened with that church's youth pastor, her former supervisor, just six months before.

While Alice's heart toward the young people never changed, from that point on she had a different heart toward her church. She felt angry. It seemed to her that the resources of the church were being used to minister, not to the wounded and broken who characterized

Jesus' ministry, but rather, to the "righteous and well," who often criticized people's association with the wounded and hurting. She felt confused. Alice had heard the admonition: "minister to people." But she had a greater sense of being squeezed into a fleshly, religious agenda preoccupied with external appearances and "goals" instead of people's real inner needs. And she felt betrayed. She realized that she was being treated as "the problem" for confronting the real problem. Alice no longer ministers at that church.

In Alice's church, as in many others like it, people with problems are viewed as unspiritual. Problems, therefore, are simply not permissible. But you can't recover from problems you aren't allowed to have. In addition, people who are wounded can't pay the bills or run the programs. Therefore, some religious places can't have too many wounded people around. Consequently, the process of recovery in the context of redemptive relationships is exchanged for the external trappings of Western churchianity. This, in part, is what the prophet meant when he said, "You are proclaiming 'peace, peace' when there is no peace."

The Fight Never Ends

Paul tells Timothy to "fight the good fight of faith" (1 Tim. 6:12). Fight really describes what we are up against.

The Greek word for fight, *agon*, means to do combat, to strive earnestly. It's where we get our word agony. The word is a present command, which means "keep fighting, keep fighting, fight and fight and fight." "Be transformed," in Romans 12:2, means: "At every point in the present, allow yourself to keep *being* transformed." Transformation is what happens to tadpoles and caterpillars over a period of time. It is a built-in phenomenon.

Colossians 2:6 says: "As therefore you received Christ Jesus the Lord, so live [walk] in Him." Here "live" or "walk" means, "At every point in the present, live the same way that you began in Christ (free—relying on what God did). Philippians 1:6 says: "I am sure that he who began a good work in you will bring it to completion at the day of Jesus Christ." The Christian life is an ongoing *process*.

Living in Process

Shame penetrates deeply. It pierces the spirit. While I know God can snap His fingers and heal someone's shame (I've even seen Him do it), most often it takes time for shame wounds to heal. Therefore, you need to know about some special processes that are common struggles for people recovering from the effects of shame. Don't fake recovery in order to earn people's acceptance or to "insure" God's approval. Since your value and acceptance is settled because of the cross, take all the time you need.

Forgiveness

Forgiveness is one of the most crucial, and often most misunderstood, steps in the healing process. Within the Christian community there is often a lack of understanding of the process of forgiveness. This misunderstanding can result in offering simplistic solutions to very difficult problems. Nothing about forgiveness is simple![1] I want you to see why forgiveness is essential.

In Matthew 18, Jesus tells a story of a king and a servant who owed him a great amount of money. The king summoned the servant in order to collect what was owed, the equivalent of ten million dollars. The slave threw himself down before the king, begged for mercy, and promised to pay if given time. The king had compassion on the slave and forgave the debt. On his way home, the servant sought out a man who owed him about eighteen dollars and demanded payment. The man threw himself down before the slave, begged for mercy and promised to pay if given time. The slave showed no mercy. Instead, he threw the man in jail. When the king found out, he called the servant back in, berated him for what he had done, and turned him over to the torturers in prison.

I want you to observe several things about this story. First, there is *no way* the servant could have paid the king. His only hope was that the king might show compassion. Therefore, his promise to pay indicated that he had no idea of the depth of his need and no concept of how much he needed the king's mercy. He was not broken. Second, because of his lack of brokenness, the servant extended no mercy or compassion to the man who *could* have paid the debt if given a little time. Third, the servant who doesn't forgive is the one who is tortured.

In practical terms it's a lot of work *not* to forgive someone. It takes a great deal of energy to keep track of someone else and carry a tally of his debt day after day, year after year. Simply put, it is less work to forgive. But it's still work.

---

[1]Heitritter and Vought, *Helping Victims of Sexual Abuse* (Minneapolis: Bethany House, 1989), 203.

While the way to be fully free from the hurt is to forgive, for many of us it's a battle (agony). We know that we should, but we can't. This adds to guilt and shame. But the reason we struggle with the issue of forgiveness at all is that we *want* to forgive but can't. Try these statements on for size: "I know I should but I don't want to and I won't." Or, "I wish I could but I can't." If you really don't want to and won't, there's not much I can say. However, if the second statement expresses your true desire, I have some good news. I believe that if you want to forgive, even though you can't right now, you will. It's a process.

There are many reasons why people have a difficult struggle with forgiveness. For people with shame, the struggle to forgive themselves is often the most difficult part of the battle. One reason some people find it impossible to forgive themselves or to know that God has forgiven them is that they keep trying to "get forgiven" for wrong things they haven't done. Others were victims of a hurt—and were doubly victimized by those who told them *they* were wrong for noticing and exposing the hurt. Some were taught that the abuse done to them was their fault. Some were taught it was unspiritual to feel, or struggle, or doubt. So these folks keep trying to get God to forgive them, and it was never God who had a problem with their pain in the first place. No wonder they can't "feel" forgiven.

The real victory in the battle of self-forgiveness is found in Colossians 2:13, 14:

> He made you alive together with Him, having forgiven us all our transgressions, having canceled out the certificate of debt consisting of decrees against us and which was hostile to us; and He has taken it out of the way, having nailed it to the cross. (NASB)

Forgiving yourself results from letting in the forgiveness that is yours for free—because of Jesus.

Words from the Bible help—but sometimes words are not enough. That's why God sent Jesus; that's why Jesus sent His Spirit; and that's why the Church is here. As Jesus says, "If you forgive the sins of any, their sins have been forgiven them" (John 20:23, NASB). It is clear from Scripture that only God can forgive sins and, indeed, it is He alone who is the forgiver. Nehemiah says, "But thou art a God ready to forgive, gracious and merciful . . ." (9:17). However, we do have the power to forgive one another through Christ and to help others experience what is true in heaven here and now. David Seamands refers to this power as "group grace."[2] If the relationships you

---

[2]David Seamands, *Healing Grace* (Wheaton: Victor Books, 1988), 178.

have in God's name don't say about you what God says about you, I recommend that you seek new ones.

Forgiving others is an important struggle in recovery, as well. I'm convinced that forgiveness toward others also comes from a sense of our being forgiven. Ephesians 4:32 says: ". . . Forgiving one another, as God in Christ forgave you." If the unforgiving servant in Matthew 18 had really understood his need and the magnitude of the forgiveness he received, there would have been a different ending to the story.

Next, coming to grips with your sense of others "owing" you is an integral part of the forgiving process. If someone owes you a "pain-debt," forgiving that person means canceling the debt. This is difficult if he won't acknowledge the pain he's caused. It's even harder if the pain-debt is great. It's harder still if you're forgiving that person in order to get some religious person or rule off your back, and you haven't *really* forgiven him in your heart. This is not forgiveness.

There's another thing that complicates the process of forgiving others. People think that if they've forgiven someone, they shouldn't be hurt anymore, or they should now be able to trust that person. This isn't always true. If you break into my house, steal my money and spend it, so you can't even pay me back, I can forgive you (cancel the debt you owe me). But it doesn't mean that I'm ready to let you into my house. And I still don't have money for groceries, so my family will have to live with the effects of what you caused, even after you're forgiven.

Matthew 18 sheds some light on this. In verses 15–17, we are told to tell our brother his fault against us, and if he listens we have gained our brother. If he doesn't we are to take someone with us to back up our effort. If he still will not listen to us, we are to take the matter to the church. If he will not listen to the church, it says "let him be to you as a Gentile and a tax collector." It's interesting that Jesus used the term "tax collector." This was a Jewish person who collected taxes for the Romans—in other words, a person who was supposed to be on your side, but who really worked for the enemy. (Does this sound like abusive families and churches?) The words "let them" in the Greek indicates that if they don't repent, you are only acknowledging what is already true, that a relationship with them is unsafe. You are not causing the problem.

I don't think forgiving others can be legislated. It is rather the result of a process of letting what God has done work in us. Try this exercise: Take two pieces of paper. On one write the name of the

152

person who has hurt you, the one who "owes" you. In addition, write what he did and the messages that the event or behavior said about you (you're defective, your feelings don't matter, etc.). On the other piece of paper write "God." Then write what is yours and who you are because of the fact that He has acted in your behalf.

Study these two papers awhile. Which one would you really rather have—God, and His affirmation of you, or the payment of your "pain-debt," (which will result in the other person suffering pain)? You can't have both. But if you choose God, then I believe forgiveness will come, even if it takes time for the truth to dawn on you as you consider what God has done for you. It will certainly take a fight (agony). But letting someone else off the hook *will* result when you realize in your heart and mind just how much God has let *you* off the hook, and from affirming that the old messages were lies, and recognizing that the person who shamed you has no power to decide *anything* about you. Only God can decide.

The Battle for Boundaries

People with shame struggle with boundary problems. That is, they aren't quite sure where their individuality begins and ends. Shame-based relationships taught them that any sense of self-preservation was selfish. Wanting what they wanted was wrong; their opinions didn't count; feeling what they felt was unimportant. No sense of appropriate boundaries were learned; no personal space was allowed. If this describes the system in which you grew up or the system in which you now live, you have no experience being *you*. In cases of abuse, boundaries were ignored, disrespected, smashed down. Because your *identity* was crushed (who you are), you learned to erect emotional boundaries (how you respond, what you do) as a matter of self-defense, for *survival.* Emotional barriers, however, result in one getting hurt over and over again because, in fact, you will tend to "let in" people who are hurtful or controlling.

As a child, Barry's parents shamed him for having feelings and opinions. He had a church that shamed him for having needs. He wasn't allowed to have personal boundaries. Now he's married to a woman who controls every area of his life. She decides who his friends are. She decides how he can spend his money. She decides the things he would "really" like to do and the places he would "really" like to go. He's miserable, but never says so outright—at least not to his wife. He's living out what he learned growing up.

Broken boundaries may also result in a strong, self-sufficient, yet lonely person who doesn't even let *safe* people come close. Maryanne's dad physically abused her mom. When her older brothers hurt Maryanne, instead of offering protection, her father offered excuses for their behavior. Through the years, she watched as her mom gradually became a nonperson. Maryanne is now a thirty-three-year-old single woman who can't seem to have a long-term relationship with a man. She's lonely and wants to have a family. When each relationship reaches a certain point, however, she pulls back and ends it abruptly. She can't even tell exactly when it's going to happen. She doesn't know why she does it, and she hates herself for doing it. Maryanne, too, is simply living out what she learned as a child.

I share these stories simply to let you know that it's okay to struggle with recovery from shame. I want you to know that your recovery will be a fight—agony. *Know* that you won't behave perfectly all of the time. *Know* that you have a right to your boundaries. *Know* that it's okay for you to expect others to respect your boundaries, and for you to confront them when they don't. Practice trusting your radar, and then take risks as you're able. Finally, *know* that even God respects your boundaries. Jesus says in Revelation 3:20, "Behold, I stand at the door and knock; if any one hears my voice and opens the door, I will come in to him, and eat with him, and he with me." Jesus wants to fellowship with us, and to help us and heal us, but He will not break down the door. He will keep knocking; you have to open the door. *You* decide if He comes in. He will respect your decision.

Spiritual Warfare

I've talked to many Christians who have been told that the terrible things that happened to them were God's way of teaching them some spiritual lesson or truth. He's made them sick, or allowed them to be raped, or put them in an abusive family to draw them closer to himself. This is a lie, and it is extremely damaging to a person. It is merely a way to put a spiritual twist to a perverted message. ("You are defective—and God allowed people to sin against you for some higher purpose that you cannot comprehend.") God can and does rescue us from terrible situations. Satan's job is to lie, steal, accuse, bind up, or weigh people down any way he can. Don't make the mistake of blaming God for what people have done against you, or for the lies that Satan promotes.

In Matthew 13:24–28 Jesus tells a story about wheat and tares. A man planted good seeds in his field. While he was sleeping, his enemy came and sowed weeds among the wheat, which were actually poisonous plants resembling wheat. When the man saw what was done, his response was *not*, "Our good friends have done this to help us grow"; or, "This has been done to keep us dependent or to draw us closer to God." His response was, "An enemy has done this!" Satan will come behind God and sow over what has been planted.

But what Satan means for evil, God means for good. In Colossians 2, it says that the cross of Christ has disarmed Satan. God can turn around the damage done by Satan. Sometimes He does it in an instant. Sometimes He does it through a therapy-and-support process that takes more time.

Every once in a while, I counsel a person who has already received all kinds of counsel that has been a great help to him. But there seems to be one small area—one block that they can't seem to get past. They always get stuck at a certain point in their progress.

In 2 Corinthians 10:4, Paul tells us that "the weapons of our warfare are not worldly but have divine power to destroy strongholds." Sometimes the strongholds that Satan erects are not simply thinking processes and behavior patterns, they are demonic strongholds in people that leave them vulnerable to Satan's lies, attacks and traps.

I think it's always a good idea to find people with whom you feel safe and ask them to pray for you. But sometimes we need those who can aggressively bring the power of God's kingdom to bear on our life and our past, and to get us beyond the blockages that hinder full deliverance. If you have ever even experimented with the occult, or been involved with someone who has, you will most certainly need someone to help who is filled with God's Spirit and experienced in pulling down the strongholds of Satan through the power of prayer.

I'm not talking about *Dear Jesus, please help so-and-so feel better.* I'm talking about *Father, pour out your Spirit in power upon this person. Do supernatural surgery on the wounds that are here. Minister your love and grace to his heart so he can begin to trust you. And Satan, in Jesus' name and by His authority, be gone! You're trespassing. You have no right to be here. This person belongs to Jesus. He's private property.*

God doesn't need experts in spiritual warfare. He responds to faith. Pray with someone with whom you feel safe and respected. Trust your spiritual radar. While you may feel uncomfortable with the process, you don't have to let someone pray for you if you feel uncomfortable with them. Satan is a trespasser. I don't expect him to play fair or repect people's boundaries. I do, however, hope that those who minister will *not* trespass or violate people's boundaries, even "in Jesus' name."

Healing Wounded Emotions

If you have a history of shame, you're going to have an ongoing struggle with emotions. The truth about emotions is that they're simply internal reactions to external situations. Larry Crabb uses the picture of the lights on a dashboard of a car to illustrate the function of emotions. Emotions can serve as a warning light telling us to take a look inside, or simply as an indication that we're on track and functioning.[3] Emotions are signals that tell us about our relationships to people, things and events. When the warning lights start flashing, the solution is *not* to disconnect them. It is important to pay attention to them in order to make wise choices about how to react.

Counseling clients have called me sometimes to ask, "I can't believe how *angry* I am. Why am I so angry?" Others call and say, "I started crying out of nowhere the other day, and I couldn't stop. Since I started looking at all this internal business, it seems that even the littlest things hook me, and I'm sad over nothing."

It's very common for someone who has kept tight reins on a feeling or on his entire emotional being to start experiencing floods of emotions as he begins to recover from his wounds. It seems that the therapeutic process causes a great deal of pain. What happens, really, is that the pain of untold wounds is simply being *found* and brought into the light where healing can take place.

Learning to pay attention to your emotions will take practice. Learning to respond to your emotions with wise decisions will also take practice. It is important all the while to stay clear on the *true nature* of the problem. The problem is not that you feel angry or sad, but rather that you've been wounded and these wounds need to be tended to and healed. Remember that the unspoken rule: "Not showing your feelings is the same as not having them" is a lie. Worse than that, it's the way to *never* find restoration and true healing.

Rage and Anger

The expression of rage is a common experience for people who live with their own sense of defectiveness, or who live with someone

---

[3]Larry Crabb, *Understanding People* (Grand Rapids: Zondervan, 1987), 184–185.

else who has shame. Anger and rage are not exactly the same. While rage looks like very strong anger, it is more closely associated with the feeling of shame.

There are three Greek words used in the New Testament to describe anger. The first is the word *perogismos*. Found in Ephesians 6:4: "Fathers, do not provoke your children to anger. . ." it means seething hostility; boiling, churning anger. Anger that doesn't come out, but festers, is *perogismos*. Unfortunately, many people think that God measures their spirituality based on the emotions they feel or don't feel. And because they may think that a repressed anger is the only acceptable kind, they are actually *striving* for this kind of anger—even though it is clear in this context that it is of a negative quality!

The second Greek word for anger is *orgay*. We see an example of this type in Ephesians 4:26, 27: "Be angry but do not sin; do not let the sun go down on your anger, and give no opportunity to the devil." *Orgay* comes the closest to representing the normal, human emotion we call anger. It's the anger that results when something that is important to you, or something to which you are committed has been threatened or damaged.

Consequently, you can *discover* some things that are important to you when you pay attention to what makes you angry. For instance: Someone at a picnic is served a bigger slice of pie than you, and you feel anger rise up. That says that pie, or food, is important to you. You get angry when someone makes fun of your clothes. That says that fashion, or clothes—or people's approval—is important to you. You get angry when someone criticizes your children or says hurtful things to them. You may be protecting your children, but you also may feel that their behavior says something about you.

You can't cease to be angry about these things simply by trying hard not to be. You need to change your mind about how important some things really are; get your priorities in order. Then when something is withheld or damaged, or you are criticized or slighted, anger will not be your first response.

You may ask, "What if what's important to me is justice, helping those in pain, meeting the needs of others, building people's self-worth, or any number of things really done in God's name and for His sake?" When these things are hindered, or when the rights of others are ignored, you *should* be angry. These are not selfish ambitions, but siding with what God feels about a situation. God gets *very* angry when people hurt His children.

The emotion of anger is not right or wrong; harmful actions induced by anger are wrong. The choices that we make when we are angry can be right or wrong. The reason the scripture cited above says not to let the sun go down on your anger is because by doing so you may allow it to seethe (become *perogismos*), which gives the enemy of our souls an opportunity to twist it or to cover the issues that are real. Seething anger will spill out later in ways we least expect.

It's not a coincidence that the Ephesians 4 passage about *orgay* anger immediately follows verse 25: "Therefore, putting away false-hood, let every one speak truth with his neighbor, for we are members one of another." In this context, it's clear that speaking the truth, keeping things in the light prevents misunderstandings and cause for unnecessary anger. Being open and honest with others minimizes occasions for sin as a result of anger.

The third Greek word for anger is *thumos*. It is an explosive-temper kind of anger, or rage. It is anger that looks bigger than the situation warrants. It is the word that is sometimes translated "out-bursts of anger" in Galatians 5:20. This kind of reaction is a result of walking by, or depending on the flesh; putting our confidence in what is natural, rather than being led by the Spirit.

There are two further comments I want to make about *thumos*. First, the Greek word translated "patience" in the fruit of the Spirit (Gal. 5:22) is *macrothumia*, or "long-to-explode anger" (sometimes translated longsuffering). This fruit results when we continue to walk by the Spirit as the Source of who we are—not from trying hard to not be angry. It is what the Spirit produces in us when we draw our sense of life, value and acceptance from Him. Second, it's important to note that in order to bear a fruit that means "long-to-explode anger," you must have the emotion of anger in the first place. Pay attention to your feelings and make wise, relationship-building choices.

The Truth Is Never the Problem

Recovering from shame is often confusing, scary, and a painstak-ing ordeal. You will be breaking the "Can't-talk" rule, bringing unspo-ken things into the light and holding others accountable for their behaviors. You'll be learning some new things, and unlearning other things. You'll learn to express your feelings and trust again. These are all things for which you've been shamed in previous relationships. Facing them now will take some real effort.

You and I *are* capable of walking in the Spirit. We don't have to live the Christian life alone, under our own steam. In fact, there's no way it can be done that way! (You've already discovered that.)

There is only *life* in the Holy Spirit, the good soil in which you are to sink your roots of identity and emotion. That life is for YOU!

14

Fighting the New Fight: Exercises

Gary and Jenny came into my office and sat, as usual, at opposite ends of the sofa. But this time something was different. They sat with their bodies semi-facing each other, instead of facing away from each other. Sometimes they even played eye games, as if they were privy to an inside joke.

"Remember the time you told us to make up those index cards? Those cards are *magical*," Jenny beamed. Gary nodded in agreement.

Several times in the past, we'd spent time talking about the problem they had telling each other about their feelings. As they got up to leave at the end of one particular session, the "index card plan" popped into my head. It seemed kind of corny, but I told them my idea anyway. (I know this is a terrible thing to do, but *later* in this chapter, I'll let you in on the idea, too.)

They agreed to try it, and their news was, "It's working." And their communication with each other continues to improve—*not* because they're trying harder. Instead, they're learning to think differently about *who* they are and what events and words really *mean*.

Ephesians 2 says we are created for good works. That means at some point, we will move from the steps of renewing our minds to seeing renewed behaviors. Obedience to God *does* matter. Bearing fruit *is* important. Romans 7:4 says: ". . . You have died to the law through the body of Christ, *so that you may belong to another, to Him who has been raised from the dead, in order that we may bear fruit for God.*"

Having healthy relationships does result in "fruitful" lives. But the difference is that the fruit is no longer the means by which we try to establish, earn, or protect our value and identity. When we learn to be consistent with who we are and with what is true about us because of Jesus, bearing fruit no longer means *producing*. It means being capable of *holding* the weight of the fruit *He* produces. Learn to be consistent with who we are and with what is true about us already— free of charge—because of Jesus.

A Matter of Consistency

The following scenario plays itself out in my office on a regular basis. Frank (or Marge) enters and slumps dejectedly in the chair. "I'm miserable," laments the client. "I know I *should* be living differently for the Lord, but I don't want to."

"Really? You don't want to do what God wants?" I half ask, half reply.

"No!" comes the response.

I push a little further. "You're sure? Look in your heart. What *do* you really want to do?"

The client sometimes answers immediately, but more often only after some serious thinking.

"Well, actually . . . I *want* to do what God wants. It's just that I don't always *do* it."

"You *want* to obey God. I thought that was true," I reply, much to the client's surprise.

"How did you know that?"

I explain how I came to my conclusion: "Well, first of all, I can't find any Christians in the New Testament who didn't *want* to do what God wanted. I find some who *didn't* do it, but none who didn't really desire to do God's will in their lives.

"The second reason is that if you didn't want to do what God wants, you wouldn't have come in for help and we wouldn't be having this conversation."

Remember the Ezekiel 36 passage? God said He would *cause* us to walk in His statutes, and see to it that we *will* be careful to observe His ordinances. How is He going to do that? It isn't by putting us under a list of rules and shaming us for not following them. Rather, He has put His Spirit in us, gotten rid of our old stony hearts, and given us new, soft hearts. Hebrews 10:16 says:

> "This is the covenant that I will make with them after those days," says the Lord: "I will put My laws on their hearts, and write them on their minds. . . ."

God's plan was to create new creations who actually *wanted* to do good things! For us to perform right behaviors on the outside is simply being consistent with the new hearts we have from God.

The passage in Romans 7:15 illustrates this. Paul says, "I do not understand my own actions. For I do not do what I want, but I do the very thing I hate." And in verse 19: "For I do not do the good I want, but the evil I do not want is what I do."

Paul is saying two things: He wants to do the good thing but doesn't do it; he doesn't want to do the bad thing but he still does it. In verse 22 he says, "For I delight in the law of God, in my inmost self. . . ." So it is not a conflict between what he knows is right and what he'd rather do. It is not a fight between "good Paul" and "bad Paul." Paul and the Holy Spirit are not at odds. The problem is that Paul's behavior is inconsistent with the heart of Paul that agrees with what God wants and even wants to do what's right!

Seizing Opportunities to Renew the Mind

There are some people whose hearts, underneath it all, are *not* willing to do what God wants. If this describes you, the next section on practicing new behaviors will not solve your problem. In fact, while learning to perform more positively might get you a lot of positive strokes from the religious crowd, it would only hide the true need. You need a heart transplant—that is, you need to cry out to God, who promises to give a new heart to all who will ask.

Then there are those who have hearts to do what God wants, (This doesn't necessarily mean doing what your church, pastor, parents, kids, denomination, or your employer wants.) But they have difficulty doing it. I want to offer some practical tools in order to bring the faith-fight down to a day-to-day level. These "renewing the mind exercises" are being given for the purpose of allowing you to practice new behaviors. They will help you to learn to act consistently with the theology you've learned concerning your gift-based identity. I'm confident that you'll be able to create more exercises to fit your particular situations as time goes on. For an entire book on the importance of renewing the mind, see *Telling Yourself the Truth*, by William Backus and Marie Chapian, Bethany House, 1980. Their main assertion is that how you believe determines how you decide to respond to events and circumstances in your life.

The "Decide-Who-Decides" Exercise

This exercise will give you practice doing two things: First, it will give you a chance to decide that behaviors, events, or opinions are not about you as a person. Second, it will give you an opportunity to decide *what* has the power to determine your value as a person—externals, or God.

When the Externals Decide

The Crime: Someone said a hurtful thing to me today, and I cried in front of everyone at work.

The Emotion: I felt humiliated.

The Desire: I wish I had never cried in front of people.

The Shame-Based "Rule": People who are acceptable, valuable, adult, capable, etc. , never cry in front of others.

The Shaming Diagnosis: Therefore, I am defective, immature, oversensitive, etc.

The Response: Quit the job, or retreat from people at work.

This person actually did quit his job. Another route someone might decide to take, however, would be to try very hard to pretend not to be hurt by the comment. Or they could just work very hard to avoid people who say or do hurtful things. The following is a way to think about what happened in a non-shaming way.

When God Decides

The New Rule: God says I'm a person who is loved, valuable and capable. No strings attached.

The Diagnosis: Therefore, even though I cried in front of people (which I hate), I am still a valuable, acceptable person.

The Response: Keep the job; tell the person I was hurt; find someone to talk to with whom I feel safe; etc.

Here's another example:

When the Externals Decide

The Behavior: The kids got out of line at the grocery store and broke some things. When I tried to correct them they ignored me—and other people were watching, too.

The Emotion: I felt embarrassed, angry, frustrated.

The Desire: I wish they never acted that way, especially in public; or I wish I knew what to do when that happens.

The Shaming Rule: Good parents don't have kids who misbehave in public; or good parents always know how to get their kids to cooperate.

The Diagnosis: Therefore, something's wrong with me. I'm a bad parent.

The Response: Yell and scream at the kids; shame them in public to get them to obey; use Bible verses on them. Give up, or play the martyr.

When God Decides

The New Rule: God says I'm loved, accepted and capable.

The Diagnosis: Therefore, even though the kids' behavior was inappropriate and I'm not sure what to do about it right now, I am still a worthwhile, valuable person.

The Response: Offer the kids reasonable consequences and follow through if they continue to act that way; attend a parenting class to gain parenting skills; look for a support group for parents so I can find out I'm not crazy and my kids aren't abnormal.

The "It's-Not-About-Me" Exercise

The purpose of this exercise is to help you learn to draw different conclusions about the meaning of what you do and things that happen. I'll give you a couple of real-life illustrations from clients, just to give you a feel for how this works.

This Is What Happened: I spent too much money at the department store.

It Seemed to Say About Me: Shame on me. I'm an irresponsible person who can't do anything right.

What It Was Really About: I made a poor choice about how to spend my money.

This Is What Happened: I ran out of gas and was late for an appointment.

It Seemed to Say About Me: What's wrong with me? I'm really stupid.

What It Was Really About: I didn't pay attention to the gas gauge; or, I tried to squeeze too many things into the limited time I had.

This Is What Happened: I hollered and screamed at the kids.

It Seemed to Say About Me: I'm really a bad parent.
What It Was Really About: I made a poor choice about how to respond.

―――――

This Is What Happened: I got fired from my job.
It Seemed to Say About Me: I am a defective, unwanted person.
What It Was Really About: My job performance didn't live up to someone's expectations; or I made a series of irresponsible choices; or someone didn't like me.

―――――

This Is What Happened: A friend of mine said some unkind things about me to some other friends.
It Seemed to Say About Me: I'm not important, and my feelings don't matter.
What It Was Really About: A friend made a poor choice concerning how he would treat me.

―――――

Sometimes, after doing the work of distinguishing between what is about *behaviors* versus what is about *me*, things still aren't clear. At such a point it might be helpful to use a diagram something like this:

What Happened	It Says About Me	God Says About Me	My Choice
Overspent	Bad person	Still loved	
Got fired	Defective	Wanted/chosen	

The "Getting-Big/Getting-Small" Exercise

I've noticed that when people experience something that is shaming, they respond in one of two directions. They either get *big* (that is, they become raging, loud, start trying twice as hard, want to debate, or try to win). Or else they get *small* (that is, they withdraw by getting quiet, by leaving, look away or down, quit what they're doing, start to cry, become people-pleasing). This exercise is simply to help you become aware of what you do, and provide a chance to think of alternatives.

How I give in to shame by getting small (in general):
   1.
   2.
   3.
   4.
   5.

How I did that this week (specifically):
   1.
   2.
   3.
   4.
   5.

How I try to overcome shame by getting big (in general):
   1.
   2.
   3.
   4.
   5.

How I did that this week (specifically):
   1.
   2.
   3.
   4.
   5.

When all was said and done, did I have more or less shame?

What are some things I could have said/done differently?

––––––––––

The "Getting-Through-the-Shame-grid" Exercise

Because people with shame have a shame-grid, things are often interpreted in a shaming way that aren't meant that way. This brings me to the index card idea I told you about at the beginning. I'll illustrate it by continuing the story of Gary and Jenny.

Gary and Jenny have a very hard time communicating. Gary comes from an alcoholic family and a shaming, abusive past. He struggles with shame and anger. Sometimes he's angry and doesn't know why. Sometimes he acts angry toward someone and he's not even angry with that person. Jenny comes from an abusive family system where anger was used as a weapon. Anger scares her to death. She learned to withdraw and keep quiet. Whenever Gary was angry, Jenny thought it meant something was wrong with her and she was going to get punished. She withdrew. Whenever Jenny withdrew, Gary thought it meant something was wrong with him and that Jenny didn't love him.

I asked each of them to make up a large index card and put a statement on each side of the card. The statement on the side of Jenny's card that faced Gary was a message to Gary; the statement on her side of the card was for her. The statement on the side of Gary's card that faced Jenny was for Jenny; the statement on his own side of the card was for him. Whenever their particular difficulty arises, which is often, they try to talk it through while holding up their cards in the appropriate direction. Here is what those "magical" cards said:

Jenny's Card (the side facing Gary)—You are a valuable person because of the cross, and I still love you and accept you, even though I don't like your behavior right now and want to withdraw.

Jenny's Card (her side)—I feel scared and am withdrawing right now, and I can't fix Gary's anger. Even then, because of the cross, I am still valuable and acceptable.

Gary's Card (the side facing Jenny)—I feel very angry right now and don't know why. What I do know is that my anger isn't about you. I love you, and you are special, because of Jesus.

Gary's Card (his side)—I feel angry right now and I don't know why. Because of Jesus, I'm still loved and accepted, even when I'm angry.

The "Who-Gets-to-Be-God" Exercise

If you struggle with believing that when something is wrong, you must have caused it, or you're supposed to fix it, try this exercise. You may realize several things while doing this task. First, you might see that you have somehow taken on the job of controlling people and matters you can't control. Second, you might get a picture of just how much time and energy you invest trying to control things over which you really have no control. And third, you may find that you'd rather just be *you*, control what you really *can* control, and let God be God over all the rest.

To do this exercise, simply choose an area in your life—how your kids act or whether your parents and spouse get along—that you think you're supposed to make turn out okay. Write it on an 8 1/2–by–11 piece of cardboard, i.e., "How my family gets along at Christmas." Next, take a 3-inch piece of masking tape, write "God" on it, and tape it on the front panel of one of your dresser drawers. Whenever you're able to believe that God is big enough to make the situation turn out the way He'd like, put the piece of cardboard in the drawer labeled "God". Whenever you are trying to make the situation work out yourself, you have to carry the cardboard around with you; if you're going to carry the problem, you have to carry the cardboard that represents it.

The purpose of this exercise is *not* to shame you by your having to carry around a goofy-looking piece of cardboard. Neither is it to get you to put the cardboard in the drawer and then *pretend* that the issue doesn't bother you anymore. It is designed simply to make you conscious of how much time you *do* spend trying to control things, and to raise the question for you of whether or not you really want to do that.

The "Fruit-of-the-Spirit" Exercise

In Galatians 5:16 Paul says: "But I say, walk by the Spirit, and you will not carry out the desire of the flesh" (NASB). "Walk by the Spirit" is the command of the text. In verses 22 and 23, he lists what results if we obey the command. "But the fruit of the Spirit is love, joy, peace, patience, kindness, goodness, faithfulness, gentleness, self-control; against such there is no law."

Notice that this is a list of the fruit of the *Spirit*. Paul isn't saying, "Try hard to love, act joyful, keep the peace, be patient, be kind, etc." It is what God's Spirit produces in and through people who boast in, rejoice in, fix their hope on, build their house upon God, or "walk by the Spirit." It is *His fruit*, not the result of your efforts to do good.

Paul gives us another list in verses 19–21: "Now the works of the flesh are plain: immorality, impurity, licentiousness, idolatry, sorcery, enmity, strife, jealousy, [outbursts of] anger, selfishness, dissensions, party spirit [factions], envy, drunkenness, carousing, and the like. . . ." Deeds of the flesh result when we walk according to the flesh, rather than according to the Spirit.

Put a list of the fruit of the Spirit on your refrigerator, on your dashboard, on top of your desk calendar, on your bathroom mirror—wherever you'll be most likely to see it. Then, the next time you are experiencing an *absence* of the fruit of the Spirit, or the *presence* of the deeds of the flesh, ask yourself, "What am I walking according to *right now*? What am I getting my life from *right now*? What am I getting my sense of value and acceptance from *right now*?" This is a diagnostic test to determine from where you are drawing your sense of value and acceptance. Remember, if you are leaning on Jesus, you *will* have the fruit of the Spirit.

And Finally . . .

After all the focus this chapter has had on acting differently, I want to re-focus, as we close, on the urgent need to keep our dependence upon God: for who you *are* and what you *do*.

"Without me," Jesus said, "you can do nothing." In chapter 13, we quoted Philippians 1:6: "And I am sure that he who began a good work in you will bring it to completion. . . ." We used the verse to illustrate that we are in a process. Now, let's remind ourselves of *whose* process it is. *God* is the one in charge of bringing the work to completion, of perfecting you. *He will do it.*

Another reminder is found in Philippians 2:13: "For God is at work in you, both to will and to work for His good pleasure." God is right now doing the work in you to change you. It's an inside job.

"What then shall we say to this?" Paul asks in Romans 8:31. In the following verses, his reply reminds us one more time to rest in God and His provision: "If God is for us, who is against us? [No one!] He who did not spare his own Son, but gave him up for us all, will he not also give us all things with him? [He will!] Who shall bring any charge against God's elect? [No one!] It is God who justifies; who is to condemn? [No one!] Who shall separate us from the love of Christ? [Nothing and no one!]"

He will freely give us all things! Love and acceptance? It is finished. The end of our shame? There is now *no* condemnation. Healing from our wounds? The process has already begun. Even fruitful lives? Yes! In 2 Corinthians 9:8 Paul says, "And God is able to make all grace abound to you, that always having all sufficiency in everything, you may have an abundance for every good deed" (NASB).

Pretty extravagant, isn't it? We have what we need to do good works for God. Ephesians 2:10 even says that good works are what we are created for. God's love for us is great and it's free. Our new identity is settled. The seal of His Spirit is on our acceptance. With practice we can "keep living by that same standard to which we have attained." Hang on to your Source. Remember what His performance on the cross says about you.

Now fight the right fight. And watch what He will do!

I'm Amazed

I have felt so much darkness, I've lived in such despair
As I've struggled with my weaknesses and the burdens that I
    bear.
But then I hear a whisper. Something says Your name.
I lift my eyes and see the cross that takes away my shame!

And I'm amazed that You love me!
I'm amazed that you care!
I'm amazed at Your compassion!
There's nothing that compares to the mercy You've shown me!
I've never known such grace!
And I want to just say "Thank You!" and tell You, "I'm amazed!"
I've had questions inside me. I've struggled with such doubt.
Could this really be the answer? Is this what life's about?
But then I look at Jesus—God's embodied love,
The unearned gift for all mankind, a pardon from above!

Could it be that You could really love me?
Do You really value me so much?
And can it be that I could even finally rest from striving
And let You heal me with Your gentle touch?!

Copyright © 1989, words and music by Dan Adler. All rights reserved. Used by permission.

For further information on tapes
on this or related family topics contact:

DAMASCUS, INC.
P.O. Box 22432
Minneapolis, MN 55422